CONSEQUENCE

CONSEQUENCE

A MEMOIR

ERIC FAIR

HENRY HOLT AND COMPANY   NEW YORK

Henry Holt and Company, LLC
Publishers since 1866
175 Fifth Avenue
New York, New York 10010
www.henryholt.com

Henry Holt® and ® are registered trademarks of
Henry Holt and Company, LLC.

Library of Congress Cataloging-in-Publication Data

Names: Fair, Eric, author.
Title: Consequence : a memoir / Eric Fair.
Description: New York : Henry Holt and Company, [2016]
Identifiers: LCCN 2015031396| ISBN 9781627795135 (hardcover) |
    ISBN 9781627795142 (electronic book)
Subjects: LCSH: Fair, Eric. | Iraq War, 2003–2011 —Personal narratives, American. |
    Military interrogation—United States. | Military interrogation—Iraq. | Linguists—
    Iraq—Biography. | Government contractors—United States—Biography. | Heart—
    Transplantation—Patients—United States—Biography. | Iraq War, 2003–2011
    —Prisoners and prisons, American. | Iraq War, 2003–2011 —Atrocities. |
    Torture—Iraq.
Classification: LCC DS79.76.F338 A3 2016 | DDC 956.7044/37—dc23
LC record available at http://lccn.loc.gov/2015031396

p. 7: lyric from "Allentown," words and music by Billy Joel, originally appearing
    on *The Nylon Curtain* album released September 23, 1982, and produced
    by Phil Ramone; recorded at A & R Recording and Media Sound Studios,
    New York City; Family Productions/Columbia

Our books may be purchased in bulk for promotional, educational, or business use.
Please contact your local bookseller or the Macmillan Corporate and
Premium Sales Department at (800) 221-7945, extension 5442, or
by e-mail at MacmillanSpecialMarkets@macmillan.com.

The names and identifying characteristics of some persons
described in this book have been changed.

First Edition 2016

Designed by Kelly S. Too

Printed in the United States of America
1 3 5 7 9 10 8 6 4 2

For my son, Carl Ferdinand Fair

For example, a person is not forgiven until he pays back his fellow man what he owes him and appeases him. He must placate him and approach him again and again until he is forgiven.

—Maimonides, the Laws of Repentance

CONSEQUENCE

ABU GHRAIB

JANUARY 2004

One of the interrogation booths at Abu Ghraib has comfortable chairs. I like to use this booth because there's a small space heater inside that cuts through the chill of the Iraqi winter. There's even a hot plate to boil water for tea, but it only works when you run an extension cord from the generator, and that prevents you from closing the door all the way. I'm interrogating an Iraqi general today, so I make the tea.

It's hard to schedule this booth because everyone wants to use it, and we're only supposed to use it when we have someone important to talk to. It's always a good thing if you're interrogating a former Iraqi army officer, especially a major or a colonel. And if you get a former general, like today, then the booth is yours for sure.

The comfortable interrogation booth is designed for an approach called change of scenery. The prisoner is supposed to think he's somewhere else; he's supposed to be tricked into thinking he's just holding a normal conversation in an office building or his living room; he's supposed to forget he's being interrogated at Abu Ghraib prison. But it's still just a plywood interrogation booth that smells like fresh-cut lumber, and it's still surrounded by the mud and the filth and the incoming mortar rounds that mark Abu Ghraib.

It's early morning—the afternoon sun is still a few hours away—so when two U.S. Army soldiers deliver the general to the booth he is shivering from the cold. I haven't had time to read the screening report, so I don't know much about him, but I'm sure his story is similar to so many of the others I've already heard. He's Shia, which means he probably commanded some poorly trained army unit that probably had more men than rifles. And he probably couldn't pay his men because he embezzled the unit's payroll in order to fund the bribes that got him promoted to general in the first place. He probably deserted during the invasion, never wanted to fight U.S. troops, and just wanted to go home and live in an Iraq free of Saddam Hussein. This is what all the former generals tell us. None of us believe it.

The report says something about the general's sons being involved in anti-Coalition activities, which doesn't make much sense because he's Shia, and it's January 2004 and the Shia haven't turned their guns on us yet. But it's hard to know what's true inside Abu Ghraib, and it's hard to make sense of anything going on in Iraq.

I'm working with one of the two good translators today. She grew up in one of Baghdad's Christian communities and moved to Michigan during high school, so unlike most translators, she's fluent in both languages. And she's fast. She doesn't wait for you to finish your sentences the way the other translators do, or ask you to repeat yourself, or waste time debating the exact meaning of a word. She talks as you talk, making the conversation seamless.

I'm supposed to collect information about the location of the general's sons, but like so many things in Iraq, it's an impossible task. He's been detained since October 2003. It's unclear what, if anything, he's done wrong. He's had no contact with his family, no information about the outside world, and no cooperation from the men who have imprisoned him. My task is to gain his trust and convince him to betray his sons.

By the time I've read the initial screening report and gathered basic background information, I've given up. I shouldn't be here. I should have quit by now. A single month at Abu Ghraib is enough to know that all of this is wrong, but I stay, in hopes of salvaging the experience and finding some way to excuse what I've done. With each day, the hole gets deeper.

I have the booth scheduled for another hour and I don't have the energy this morning to start on someone new. So I take the time to ask the general about his life and learn what I can about Iraq. I do this with most prisoners, whether they have intelligence value or not. When I write the report, I'm supposed to call this the approach phase. I'm supposed to be building rapport. Some interrogators talk about how good they are at this, how they develop relationships with prisoners and come to some sort of understanding, opening lines of communication that will eventually produce good intelligence.

It's all bullshit. This is Abu Ghraib prison. The Iraqis hate all of us.

As I talk to the general about the village where he grew up, his service in the Iran-Iraq War, and how much he loves his sons, I ignore the memories from the previous night, when I interrogated a young man in one of the uncomfortable interrogation booths. I made him stand with his arms in the air until he dropped them in exhaustion. He lied to me, said he didn't know anything about the men he was captured with or the bomb that had been buried in the road. So I hurt him. Now I'm in a decent room serving decent tea and acting like a decent man. The comfortable interrogation booth is all I need to convince myself that the general and I are enjoying this conversation. I've fallen for my own stupid trick. When I pour the tea and turn up the heater, I complete the illusion.

As we drink our tea, the translator starts a conversation with the general about what it was like growing up as a Christian in Iraq and how her Muslim neighbors always took good care of her. I was an Arabic linguist in the Army, and while my language skills have faded, I understand enough to allow the translator to steer the conversation for a bit. The general says he was never very religious, but as he gets older he attends Friday prayers more often. The translator seems to like him. I do, too. I pretend the general feels the same way about me.

I talk about growing up in Pennsylvania and attending a Presbyterian church as a boy and how hearing the call to prayer from the mosques of Baghdad reminds me that I should be praying to my god more often. "No, no," the general says in English. "Not a different god. Same god. Same god." He points at both the translator and me. "We are same god."

The general and I are excited to discover that we are both former police officers, so we talk about how hard that job could be and how police officers are the ones everyone turns to when something goes wrong. He says he always thought about going back to police work, but now something is wrong with his kidneys and he has to take too many kinds of medicines.

I take too many kinds of medicines, too. I have heart failure. It cost me my job with the police department. I shouldn't even be in Iraq, but I'd been a soldier once, and I felt an obligation to be part of the war, so I lied during the physical and became a contractor. "Besides," I say to the general, "why do doctors only send healthy men to war?"

This makes the general laugh. He hates his doctors, too. He grabs his belly and shakes it and says the medicines make him gain weight. He says I look too healthy to be sick. But he says I should do what my doctors tell me. American doctors are much better than Iraqi doctors. I am too young. I have more life to live.

He asks more questions about where I am from. I shouldn't be letting him do this, but I've already lost control of the interrogation. I look to the translator. She says the general likes me and I should just keep talking and see what happens. I talk about Bethlehem, Pennsylvania, and the steel mill there, which just went bankrupt. He doesn't understand what I mean by "rust belt," so we talk about the dying industries and the closing factories. He says this is just like Iraq: no jobs and no place to work. There is no place for men to feel like men.

The general asks me about my time in the Army. I tell the general I was a sergeant, not an officer like him. He finds this hard to believe, because most enlisted Iraqi soldiers have little or no education. I tell him that I was a paratrooper, and talk about my time learning to jump out of planes and patrol the swamps and forests of American military bases. Training was difficult, but it helped us become better soldiers. The general gets excited when I mention that I served with the 101st Airborne Division. He says his unit was like mine. He mentions the Hammurabi Division.

But now that he is comfortable and the conversation is easy, the general has just confessed to a lie. The Hammurabi Division was a part of Saddam Hussein's Republican Guard, trusted troops who were expected to defend Baghdad to the death. But they didn't. They surrendered and blended back into the populace. The general hasn't mentioned this before, and while it's not critical intelligence information, it's a slip that is enough to change his status at Abu Ghraib: he's now a high-value prisoner. His interrogations will be more frequent. They won't be conducted in the booth with comfortable chairs anymore.

But I pretend not to notice his mistake. I steer the conversation away from the military and avoid subjects related to the war. I want to re-create the world we were just in, a world where I am kind to an old man and he says nice things about the way I speak Arabic. I don't want to admit that the general is probably trying to manipulate me, fishing for common ground and finding ways to relate. But our discussion about church and mosques and calls to prayer has reminded me about where this journey to Abu Ghraib started, and how far away I am from where I had hoped it would go.

At Abu Ghraib, I have put my hands on detainees, shoved them into walls, and turned a blind eye when others did the same. I have walked the halls of the hard site where the harshest interrogations take place, and averted my gaze from one of the most appalling chapters in American history. But as I talk to the general, I pretend there will be a day when these memories have faded, when all I remember are good conversations with Iraqi generals and the decent tea I learned to serve. I can go back to my Presbyterian church and pray to my god. But that's an illusion, too.

As the hour with the general comes to a close, I'm convinced I've developed a genuine rapport. It's worth making one final effort to ask about his sons.

I give the general a speech about the future of Iraq, a speech that, by now, I've given to many detainees, about how we need honest and brave men willing to carve out a new future for Iraq. It doesn't matter why America invaded Iraq or what mistakes were made along the way; all that matters is we move forward and stay on the path. The right choices will build a strong foundation for a new Iraq. The wrong ones will have consequences.

The general is nodding in agreement, so I return to the issue of his sons. In an effort to establish common ground, I tell him I have kids, too. I don't. But when I do, this speech will haunt me.

I say that someday our sons will ask us about what we did here. We will tell them that we made the right choices, the difficult choices, and they will be proud of us.

The general is crying. Even the translator, who has three sons of her own, is beginning to tear up. I'm tempted to think I've gained the general's trust, that he's willing to provide information about his sons, and that he thinks of me as a decent man.

None of this is true. Instead, I've succeeded only in making all of us homesick.

I deliver the final part of the speech in my own broken Arabic, but the translator still repeats my words. The general hears both my heavily accented Arabic and the translator's perfect Iraqi dialect. It comes to him as an echo.

I say a new day for Iraq is here. We must seize it. We must save Iraq. We must do what is right. For our sons! For our sons!

"God willing," he sobs. "For our sons, for our sons."

1

In Pennsylvania, Bethlehem Steel is dying. I grow up watching it die. It built naval guns for World War I and Liberty ships for World War II. It built the Golden Gate Bridge and the New York City skyline. But the country eventually lost its thirst for steel. In Bethlehem, there were too many pensions, too many vice presidents, too many corner offices. In elementary school, we learn words like "pig iron," "coke," "limestone," and "slag." But we also learn words like "Kraut steel" and "Jap steel." We watch neighbors lose their jobs. We put on a spring musical and sing a Billy Joel song.

Out in Bethlehem they're killing time

Like the fathers in the song, my grandfathers fought the Second World War. My father received a deferment for Vietnam. In my boyhood, he tells me stories about how the Army was going to train him to fly helicopters, but they passed him over because he was a public school teacher with a daughter on the way. He says it's a good thing he never flew helicopters, because at the time "they were knocking those things down with tennis balls." The image fascinates me. I ask him to tell these stories often.

My mother is a substitute teacher. On the days she teaches, I eat breakfast at Steve Kave's house. Steve's father works at the steel mill, where he is forced to share a single job with two other steelworkers. The plant allows them to split the salary. It's the only way to keep them all employed. Mr. Kave only has one leg. He lost the other in Vietnam when they shot down his helicopter.

When I'm sick, I stay home from school at the Kaves' house. I lie on their couch and watch TV. In 1981, I watch Ronald Reagan get shot. In 1983, I watch paratroopers ride on helicopters and invade Grenada.

On Sundays, we attend the First Presbyterian Church of Bethlehem, Pennsylvania. The church is large and wealthy. Eugene Grace, the CEO of Bethlehem Steel till 1945, and chairman of the board until 1957, attended services here. Employees looking to climb the ladder poured into the church pews on Sunday mornings in hopes of being seen by Mr. Grace.

As a boy, I don't know much about Presbyterians. I know we baptize babies and I know we aren't allowed to clap in church. I never see anyone carrying a Bible. But all the men wear suits and ties. A talented choir makes beautiful music. When they finish, there is silence. Occasionally someone tries to applaud. Older members, including my grandmother, shake their heads and say, "We are here to worship God, not the choir."

My grandparents, Dorothy and Phillip Fair, are well known at First Presbyterian Church. My grandfather worked as a reporter in Altoona, Pennsylvania, after the war. Multiple sclerosis has confined him to a wheelchair. There is always someone willing to help unload him from the car on Sunday mornings, or wheel him up the ramp, or escort him into the sanctuary and help him page through the weekly bulletin. My grandmother works in the visitors' booth between services. She serves coffee and tea and holds long conversations with people she's never met before. Then she introduces us to these people and talks to them as if they are old family friends.

We visit my grandparents on Saturday mornings. I'm allowed to ride my grandfather's wheelchair down the ramps that have been installed throughout the house. The VA hospital has provided my grandfather with a remote-controlled television. It's the first one I've ever seen. The remote has two large buttons. You can only turn the channel one way, so you have to cycle through all thirteen channels to get back to the beginning. I sit and press the button and watch the channels change as my parents and grandparents sit in the other room and talk about family.

My grandmother tells stories about the MacFarlanes, Campbells, and Burds. She talks about the deep Scottish roots and how important the Presbyterian church has been to the family. There are drawers full of photo albums with black-and-white portraits of well-dressed men. Colonel Burd posing with his unit at Gettysburg in 1898 as they prepare to deploy to the Spanish-American War. A photo of William Burd standing in front of his Presbyterian church in 1902 after preaching one of his sermons. And there is a collection of letters from James MacFarlane, written during his service in the Civil War.

I grow up listening to my grandmother's tales. I grow up learning that I come from a long line of Presbyterians who valued their faith and marched off to war.

In 1983, I start sixth grade. I am small and slightly overweight. I'm not fat, but my mother buys my jeans in the husky section at the Hess's department store in Allentown. I am slow. At Nitschmann Middle School, we take the Presidential Physical Fitness Test. My father tells me it was President Eisenhower's idea. Eisenhower was unimpressed by the fitness level of World War II draftees, so he decided it would be a good idea to make sixth-graders do pull-ups. I can't do pull-ups. I just hang on the bar with my face to the wall. My fellow students sit behind me on the gym floor and laugh. There is also a shuttle run and some sort of stretching exercise. I fail to impress on those events as well.

At Nitschmann we have special activity days. Students are allowed to choose an activity that interests them. I choose a class about statistics and board games. Mostly we just play Risk. A popular girl from the majorette squad is in the class, too. We start to become friends. A few weeks later, during homeroom, Principal Kartsotis announces my name over the school's intercom. He recites other names, too. They belong to the kids who don't play sports and who buy their jeans in the husky section. Principal Kartsotis tells us that we will be removed from our special activities classes and enrolled in a fitness program. The gym teacher, Mr. Lindenmuth, makes us run laps and hang from the pull-up bar.

At home, I remember being told that I shouldn't feel embarrassed. At Nitschmann, I remember meeting the majorette in the hallway a few days later and lying to her about why I couldn't play Risk anymore. I remember spending much of that year being sent to the guidance counselor's office for crying during school.

I spend my weeks at Nitschmann Middle School looking forward to Sunday mornings at First Presbyterian Church. The chimes of a large bell in the towering white steeple greet us as we arrive. I like the sound my dress shoes make on the slate floor in the narthex. Ushers in crisp dark suits, with white shirts, escort us down the aisle and hand me a program. I am twelve years old, but they call me sir, or young man, or, on occasion, Mr. Fair. They offer a firm handshake. My family lets me sit in the aisle seat, where I have a better view of the choir and the pulpit. If an adult sits down in front of me they always turn around to ask whether I can see.

The pastor at First Presbyterian is handsome and popular. He shakes my father's hand and points at my tie: "Attaboy." He played quarterback on his college football team and he often talks about the Pittsburgh Steelers during his sermons. There are no theatrics during the sermon. His voice is strong, but there is no yelling. He stands nearly still in the pulpit, removing his glasses to emphasize certain points. The sermons are almost always about love and the need to reach out to those in pain. I watch as the adults in the sanctuary sit nearly still. Occasionally they nod their heads, or write something down on the back of the bulletin, but they are completely silent. It is the one time during the week when I feel safe.

In 1986 I make the transition to Liberty High School. In ninth grade, we study world cultures. There is a week about Vietnam. Mr. Gentry, a history teacher at the school, comes to class and talks about his service in the Army. One day he goes drinking in Saigon. As they stumble outside, a young boy shoves his hand in Mr. Gentry's pocket. He thinks the boy is trying to rob him, so he grabs the hand and yanks it out. The boy has a grenade in his hand. Mr. Gentry's friends attempt to get control of the grenade but the boy won't let go. They overwhelm the boy and pin him to the ground. Someone kills the boy. They don't want to pry the dead fingers loose so they saw off the arm and toss it into the air. It detonates and sprays the men with shrapnel. Mr. Gentry shows us the scars. He says, "I think about that boy a lot."

There are twenty-five hundred students at Liberty. The school consists of three main buildings, the oldest of which was built in 1918. It has marble staircases and large dark hallways. A labyrinth of overpasses and concrete walkways connects the three main buildings. Between classes, students congregate on these overpasses and walkways, creating choke points where larger students threaten smaller students. One day, in ninth grade, I accidentally step on the heel of a larger student. The student says something threatening. I try to walk away, but he approaches from behind and strikes me on the back of the head with an oversized textbook. The blow leaves me nauseated. The crowd makes room; larger students cheer while smaller ones look on in silence.

At home, I cry. My father is a history teacher at Liberty. He offers to intervene. I don't know how to survive high school, but I know I can't ask my father to protect me. I tell my father he should let me handle this on my own. He hands me a roll of quarters and shows me how to make a fist around them. He says, "Last resort." I am terrified. The next day I am forced to navigate the crowded overpass again. My father is standing guard in the center of the crowd along with a group of students from his senior history class. My father and I have been friends ever since.

In October 1986, the Boston Red Sox lose the World Series to the New York Mets. The next day, I wear a Red Sox hat to school. A boy wearing a Mets hat beats me badly for this, while his friends stand by and laugh. I go home and cry again, but not in front of my father. My older sister takes notice and forces me to tell her what happened; then she calls some of her friends. One of them plays linebacker for the Liberty High School football team. She tells him to handle it. The next day, the Mets fan approaches me in the hallway and apologizes. His friends do the same. My sister and I have been friends ever since.

For the next two years, before my father drives me to school, I drink Pepto-Bismol with breakfast. The memory of the mint-chalk flavor lingers into adulthood. At night, I'm too afraid to concentrate. I struggle in Mr. Wetcher's honors-level algebra class. He returns our exams in order of performance, saving the best grades for last. My tests are handed back first. Eventually, Mr. Wetcher drops me into a lower-level algebra section. He announces my departure to the class, then walks me down the hall and delivers me to the new teacher. The new class is seated alphabetically. Almost everyone is forced to move to a new desk. There are loud complaints as they shuffle their belongings and drop their books. Mr. Wetcher wishes me luck.

I seek refuge at church. Don Hackett, the youth pastor at First Presbyterian, is the first adult who allows me to call him by his first name. Don takes me under his wing. In the mornings, before school, he picks me up and takes me to breakfast. He challenges me to memorize Scripture, holding me accountable to a strict weekly schedule. He asks me to help teach the sixth-graders on Wednesday nights and makes me give the weekly announcements, forcing me to face my insecurities about performing in front of large groups. He teaches me how to be properly prepared for meetings and stresses the importance of public speaking.

As I continue to struggle in school, my parents look for ways to turn me around. Grades matter most, and mine are terrible. There are long, loud arguments about trying harder and not making excuses. I tell my father that some of my other friends are struggling, too. He tells me to find smarter friends. I take my frustrations out on my parents. I start stealing money from my father's dresser drawer. When he catches me, there are more loud arguments about consequences and accountability.

My father forces me to take on a paper route as punishment for stealing the money. In the mornings, before school, I ride my bike to a neighborhood apartment complex and deliver the Bethlehem *Morning Call*. Every month, I am required to collect money from my customers. I can hear my customers through the thin walls of the apartment complex saying, "It's the paper boy, don't open the door."

In the 1980s, Bethlehem Steel loses more than a billion dollars. There is talk about a brief return to profitability, but only after a significant portion of the workforce is laid off. Unemployment brings crime, and Bethlehem is not immune.

One morning, after finishing my route, I return to the light pole where I lock my bike. There is a large man removing my front wheel and rifling through the storage bag on the backseat where I keep my collection book. When he sees me, he begins to walk away, taking the wheel with him. I say, "That's my bike." He turns, takes a few steps toward me, and says, "Well, you shouldn't leave it out here unattended." I begin to walk away, but he follows. There is a fire station across the street. In a panic, I wheel what's left of my bike to the front door and ring the bell. No one answers. I ring it again, and again, and again, not knowing what the firemen can do, but hoping they'll at least let me come inside. The man with my wheel eventually leaves, but the firemen never answer.

When I get home, my father calls the police. The police officer is large and intimidating. He sits down at the dining room table and listens to my story. He laughs when I talk about no one answering the bell at the firehouse. He says, "Fucking firemen." My dad and I laugh, too. The police officer says I did everything right. He says they know about the apartment complex. It has a reputation for this type of thing. They probably won't be able to catch the guy, but they'll certainly be looking for him.

The next morning I walk to the apartment complex to deliver the papers. I'm scared. I arrive to find that same police officer parked across the street. He stays until I finish the route.

1.1

Eventually high school becomes a better place. I can do pull-ups. I have friends. I begin dating a girl from church. She French-kisses me in the church parking lot.

I don't think I'm supposed to be kissing girls at church, so I don't tell Don. But it isn't difficult for him to find out from others what's going on, so he pulls me aside and talks about how it's best to avoid shallow relationships at my age.

I break up with the girl from church, but only for a short time. I like the way she looks, I like the way it feels to be next to her, and I like the things she does to me in the church parking lot. And there are other girls too, including ones who don't go to church. But Don's words mean a great deal to me, so I do not have sex. I'm afraid to do something that can't be undone.

In 1988, during my sophomore year in high school, I begin attending youth group meetings on Sunday nights. But instead of the quiet and reserved services I've come to love in the sanctuary, there are drums, guitars, and lots of clapping.

Don does not always attend the meetings on Sunday nights. When he doesn't, volunteer leaders, college students mostly, talk about Jesus and being born again. One Sunday night, a volunteer leader stands up in front of the group and tells us about how Jesus died. He tells us to stand up and lift our arms in the air. When some of us start to struggle, he yells at us to hold our positions. He says we could never handle what Jesus did for us on the cross. You can't breathe, so you have to hold your weight up with your arms, and eventually they give out and you suffocate to death. I don't think that I had anything to do with Jesus dying in this horrible way. I don't think I would ever ask someone to do something like this. I don't think I need to be saved.

When I attend the Sunday night youth group meetings, I sit in the back, stay silent, and watch others clap their hands and talk about being born again.

1.2

In December 1989, the United States invades Panama. In history class, Mr. Deutsch makes us read newspapers. I read an article in the *New York Times* about the 82nd Airborne Division and its role in the invasion. The article says the 82nd Airborne represents the best the country has to offer. They are men who lead by example and do not draw attention to themselves. They are quiet professionals who do impressive things like kill bad guys and feed starving refugees all on the same day.

By 1990, my senior year in high school, I no longer take beatings under the overpass. I take honors-level courses and participate in the high school activities that my guidance counselor says will make me look more impressive on my college applications. I apply to a variety of small liberal arts colleges in Pennsylvania and New England, but I also spend time in the Army recruiting office. The church has played a critical role in my life. Men like Don Hackett offered a safe place where I could grow and mature. I want to offer that same protection to others. I want to be like the police officer who showed up at my paper route. I want to be a quiet professional who saves starving refugees.

Don says a calling is a way of defining our choices in life. We don't hear a voice or have a vision. Instead, we rely on those we trust to help us make good decisions. When the process is done properly, we honor God with the choices we make. I tell Don that I feel called to law enforcement. Don tells me that I can't just make that decision on my own. He says you have to follow a path, not create one.

Don and I talk about the difficulty of being a soldier while still following Christian tenets such as turning the other cheek and loving your enemy. But Don says there are different ways to love your enemy. He says the world can be a difficult place. He says sometimes God calls us to do what is necessary to protect people. I ask him about war. I ask him about killing. He says, "Sometimes it's okay to lie to evil."

1.3

During my childhood, when my father wasn't grading papers or preparing lesson plans, he was working a second job stocking shelves and manning the register at Pennsylvania State liquor stores. My mother eventually turned her substitute-teaching position into a full-time job teaching high school biology. My parents are supportive of my decision to pursue a career in law enforcement, but they insist that I attend college first. They are adamant about the importance and value of a four-year degree. They have saved their money for a reason. Before I graduate high school, they agree to shoulder the entire cost of my education.

I receive a number of acceptance letters from small Pennsylvania colleges. But there is also an acceptance letter from Gordon College, a small Christian school in Wenham, Massachusetts, so I attend a weekend for prospective students.

I spend the weekend with Roy Carson, a Gordon College sophomore. I go to class with him, eat in the dining facility, and sleep in his dorm room. Roy is fat. He sweats constantly. His skin leaks grease. His slick hair sticks to the pimples on the back of his neck. He talks constantly. He won't let you say anything. He barely pauses to take a breath.

I am embarrassed to be seen with Roy, but Gordon College

students are not. They stop and take time to talk to him. They listen intently as he rambles on and interrupts anyone who tries to speak. They shake his hand or give him a hug. They ask him to sit with them at dinner and invite him to evening gatherings. I can picture Roy Carson as a student at Nitschmann Middle School. And I can picture him failing the presidential fitness test. But I don't think anyone at Gordon would care.

The curriculum and special religious focus at Gordon College hold no special interest for me. I don't care about learning economics from a Christian perspective or hearing a biblical viewpoint in a science class. Instead, I think about the terrible days at Liberty High School. I think about the beatings and the sleepless nights and how hard it was to concentrate in Mr. Wetcher's algebra class. If my parents are going to force me to go to college, I want to go somewhere safe. I enroll as a student at Gordon College.

1.4

In the fall of 1990, I spend my first semester at college adjusting to life in a Christian dorm. Wood Hall is the oldest dorm on campus. Half of the building is reserved for male students, the other half for female. There are visiting hours for the opposite sex on the weekends, but only in the evenings. While there is no prohibition against dating, students of the opposite sex are forbidden to make public displays of affection. Some students push the envelope by holding hands. The girl from First Presbyterian Church visits me on campus and we push the envelope even further.

I meet students from a variety of Christian backgrounds. Many attended private Christian high schools that funnel them into Christian colleges like Gordon. Some of them talk about the dangers of a secular education and the effect it can have on faith. During a class on the New Testament, students debate the origins and efficacy of infant baptism. A student stands up and says anyone who was

baptized as an infant needs to be baptized again. There is some dis-
agreement, but most students concede that babies can't accept Christ.
Someone else tries to argue that if you aren't baptized as an adult
you aren't really Christian, but the professor says this is going too far.

The sentiment reminds me of the Sunday night youth group
meetings at First Presbyterian Church, where youth leaders taught
us that you needed to be saved to belong. I am uncomfortable, but I
stay silent. I want to be safe at Gordon, I don't want to be a target
again, so I avoid defending anyone my classmates say doesn't belong.

1.5

The week before Thanksgiving of my first semester at Gordon,
someone hands me a pamphlet advertising a support group for students from non-Christian homes. At the bottom, there is a series of
questions.

> Do you pray regularly with your family?
> Do you read Scripture with your family?
> Do your parents speak the name of Jesus?
> Were you baptized as an adult?

I answer no to these questions. I tally up my score. The score says
it is possible I do not come from a Christian home.

I attend the support group meeting along with other students
who may not come from Christian homes. I meet two other Presbyterians. The leader of the group gives a talk about visiting churches
where the congregants don't even carry Bibles. He says this is very
dangerous. He says there are houses throughout America where the
name of Jesus is never mentioned.

At Thanksgiving, I return home and show Don the pamphlet. I ask
him if I should be concerned about my family's Christianity. My

parents never talked about issues of faith around the dinner table. My grandmother never talked about Jesus. Instead, my family talked about history, biology, and books. I ask Don whether it's possible that my family isn't Christian at all.

Don is furious. He says, "You don't choose God. God chooses you." Don reminds me of all the Scripture I've memorized and all the verses about fools and the foolish things they say. He reminds me that I've told him I feel called to protect people, but I won't even defend my own family. He tells me my grandmother is the kindest and quietest person any of us have ever met. He says, "That's the voice you should be listening to."

1.6

In January 1991 I sit in the common room at Gordon College and watch the beginning of Operation Desert Storm. Someone says they heard the draft will be implemented by the end of the week. Someone else says students from Christian colleges will be exempt. Students talk about just war theory and the writings of Augustine. No one talks about joining the military.

I think about the recruiters from Bethlehem. I think of Mr. Kave and Mr. Gentry. I think of helicopters being shot down with tennis balls and of young children sticking grenades into the pockets of American soldiers. I think of the quiet professionals of the 82nd Airborne Division who feed starving refugees. I think of students skipping out on chapel. I think of long discussions about infant baptism and the pamphlet from the support group that suggested I might not come from a Christian home.

In Bethlehem, Don offers me a summer job working at the church as an associate in youth ministry. I spend the summer leading Bible study groups for middle school students and taking them to amusement parks and baseball games. I organize a popular Frisbee match on Sunday afternoons on the church's front lawn. I lead a camping trip into the Pocono Mountains and I organize work crews to assist the local soup kitchen. In the Middle East, U.S. troops are celebrating an overwhelming victory against Iraq. But the Kuwaiti oil fires continue to burn, and there is talk about Saddam Hussein hiding his weapons. And I'm ashamed not to be involved.

1.7

In the fall of 1991, back at Gordon College, I take a class on Romans and Galatians. The professor, William Buehler, a veteran, has taught theology since the 1960s. During the first class of the semester, Buehler gives a lecture on the dangers of the modern church. He complains about overhead projectors: "When I walk into a church service with an overhead projector, I turn around and walk back out." He also talks about guitars and drum sets. He says, "And, for God's sake, there should be no clapping in church. It's not a Broadway musical."

The first chapter of Romans talks about men committing shameless acts with other men, which leads to a debate about homosexuality. Some quote other parts of Romans and say homosexuality is being compared to murder. They say Paul may even be suggesting we put homosexuals to death. As in the conversation about baptizing babies, I choose to stay silent. I avoid becoming a target.

Buehler says the comparison of gays to murderers is the type of thinking he finds at churches with overhead projectors. He encourages us to read through Romans and Galatians before deciding we know what Paul thinks. He tells us to grow up and see the world. "Join the military," he says. "And while you're at it, transfer out of Gordon, get a real education."

In 1992, after three semesters at Gordon College, I transfer to Boston University. I doubt Buehler was seriously encouraging us to leave Gordon. But Gordon showed me something essential about how the church could move away from its responsibility to care and protect and instead choose to condemn and accuse. I was too afraid to confront it, so I left.

I move into a Boston University dorm on Beacon Street over Christmas break in 1992. I arrive a few days early, to attend an orientation program designed for transfer students. The room is a double but there is only one bed. With the help of a janitor, I find the other bed stacked in a closet down the hall. I clear space in the room and carve out my territory. I hear footsteps, then keys, then the door. Mike, my new roommate, curses and throws his bags. He says the school promised him he wouldn't be getting a roommate. He has a ton of work to do this semester and he can't afford to have someone in the way. My Gordon College sweatshirt is hanging on the back of my chair. He says, "Gordon College? Oh, fuck no." He calls the housing office. They deny his request for a single room. He throws the phone and leaves the room.

His girlfriend moves in with us. At night they are loud. In the mornings, Mike says, "Are you sure you don't want to look for a new room?" I spend a great deal of time in the library trying to hear God. I take an introductory philosophy class and read *The Myth of Sisyphus,* by Albert Camus.

Camus says we cannot know God. In the dorm, my roommate sees me reading the book and says, "I love Camus. Fucking genius." On Sunday morning, I wake up early to go to church. I open the window and turn on the lights. I bang drawers and drop coins on the floor. The girlfriend climbs out of bed, naked, and says, "Think of this when you're trying to pray."

Mike and I eventually become friends. We return to our dorm room after dinner and watch the evening news together. One evening, there is a report about changing attitudes in the military. There is talk in Washington about finding ways to allow gay men and women to serve in uniform. Mike is surprised to hear me say something supportive about this.

In the coming weeks, Mike introduces me to his friends. Some are gay. Some are not. None of them go to church. In the evening, after class, I walk back to the dorm along Commonwealth Ave with Mike's girlfriend. She says, "We just thought you were one of the bad guys."

1.8

In the summer of 1993, Army Rangers are dying in Somalia. I'm working at First Presbyterian Church again, playing Frisbee, going to amusement parks, and teaching Bible study. I visit the Army recruiters on Stefko Boulevard in Bethlehem. I don't tell my parents this time. I don't need permission to enlist. President Clinton withdraws troops from Somalia. Wars don't last long anymore.

I move off campus for my senior year. I take a class on World War I. I read about the generation of 1914, trench warfare, and mustard gas. I read *All Quiet on the Western Front* and write a paper about Wilfred Owen.

I read an article in the *Boston Globe* about a war on the streets of Boston. The article mentions the infamous 1989 Charles Stuart case and how it exposed racism in the city. Charles Stuart, a white man, drove his wife to the Mission Hill neighborhood and murdered her. He blamed the crime on a black man wearing a hooded sweatshirt. People in Boston thought of Mission Hill and the Bromley-Heath housing project as places filled with bad black men, so they believed the story was true. Police tore Mission Hill apart. They arrested a black man. The case fell apart. It turns out Charles Stuart was in debt. He murdered his wife for the insurance payment. Charles Stuart eventually committed suicide by jumping off a bridge. The police released the innocent black man from custody. But in the early 1990s, as I read about a war on the streets of Boston, people still think of Bromley-Heath and Mission Hill as bad places full of bad people.

A friend of mine from Gordon who is studying urban ministry rents an apartment in Roxbury with three other men on the condition that there are always two whites and two blacks in the apartment. He wants to prove that blacks and whites can live together. When one of the roommates gets married and moves out, I'm offered one of the white rooms. In the evenings I work in downtown Boston, delivering packages to law firms and tax lawyers. I work late into the night. Afterward, I ride my bike back to Roxbury through neighborhoods where my roommates tell me not to ride my bike.

The apartment is often engulfed in a concert of police sirens and shouting matches. I eavesdrop on domestic disputes from the back porch and avoid the drunks and addicts as I ride my bike to campus. I watch the news and hear about a shooting that took place a few blocks away. At night, the four of us sit out back and talk about Boston. Jay, one of the black roommates, works for a Christian organization called Young Life. Some of the kids who attend Young Life in Roxbury are former gang members. Jay says the gang members tell him the difference between the Boston police and the Metro police. He says there are black Boston police officers, but there are no black Metro police officers. He says no one cares when the Boston police show up, but the Metro guys mean business. He says, "You don't fuck with the Metro guys."

Jay is a large man. He was a star athlete in high school and was recruited to play basketball in college. He always has friends at the apartment. My other roommates tell me that these friends are associated with the gangs in Bromley-Heath and Mission Hill. Some of them come from opposing gangs, but when they're with Jay, everyone is safe.

One evening, Jay and I are the only two in the apartment. He says, "Why are you always avoiding me? Why are you always leaving when I show up?" I tell him about wanting to be a police officer. I assume black people don't want to be police officers. I don't tell Jay this. He says, "If you want to protect people in this city, you're going to have to learn to hang out with black people."

On Sundays I begin to attend a Pentecostal church in Dorchester with the guys from the apartment. We arrive early and set up metal folding chairs and the overhead projector. There are guitars, drums, and clapping. Many of the congregants are black. After the sermon they gather in the aisle and share the peace. They mingle and hug and say, "Peace be with you." This is something Presbyterians don't do. On the way home I tell my roommates that I'm just not a "share the peace" kind of guy. Jay says, "Maybe you're just meant to be a Metro police guy."

In the fall of 1993, my senior year at Boston University, I call the Boston Police Department and enroll in the testing program. I've done what my parents asked and earned my degree, but I haven't lost interest in law enforcement. There is a civil service test in January. There are more than seven thousand applicants. I earn a perfect score, but it's not enough. Applicants with "preference points" are elevated on the list. I call the recruitment office and ask for advice. "Join the Army, get veterans' preference, and we'll see you when you get back."

1.9

In 1994, I graduate from Boston University and return home to Bethlehem. The steel company isn't making anything anymore. The newspapers write about decentralization. The blast furnaces go quiet. Paratroopers invade Haiti. My father calls and says that CNN has come to Liberty High School to ask questions about the intervention. They want the perspective of a working-class town, and they're going to interview my father's history class. He asks me to videotape the event.

I sit down with Don and tell him about the civil service test in Boston. He says, "When God closes a window, he opens a door." I tell him I'm joining the Army. I tell him it's a necessary step to becoming a police officer.

On Sundays, I visit my Presbyterian grandmother after church. When I tell her about joining the military, she talks about the day my grandfather left for the Army. She hands me a black-and-white photograph of him in uniform. He's waiting for the train, heading back to base after a short furlough. My two-year-old father stands next to him, hanging on his leg. She talks about how everyone thought World War II was necessary. They all felt they were doing the right thing, that it was good they were marching off to war, that it was good that everyone was doing their part. Then she says, "Of course, we didn't actually know what they were going through. We didn't actually know what they were doing over there. If we did, I'm not sure how we would have felt."

My grandmother sounds sad, but she quickly changes the subject. She starts telling the stories about family and all the places they have come from. She pulls out the enormous Bible that once sat on the lectern in the church at Spruce Creek. It was published in 1874. She remembers playing in her grandfather's office and being told to be quiet because he was working on a sermon. She tells me that the Bible is mine. She writes my name on an index card and slips it into the cover page. I can't help but sense a certain disappointment that I haven't followed in her grandfather's footsteps.

In 1995 I open the door at the Army recruiting station on Stefko Boulevard. Friends, to include Mr. Gentry, have advised me to apply to Officer Candidate School. This is the path most college graduates take into the military. Officers lead a much better life in the Army than enlisted personnel. They are paid better, live in better housing, and outrank every enlisted soldier. Enlisted soldiers are forced to do menial jobs like raking leaves and cleaning toilets. They are housed in the barracks alongside other soldiers and receive half the salary of an officer. But enlisted soldiers, unlike officers, can choose their own training school and select their own career path. I want to control my own path. I want to be a military policeman, so I enlist.

I take the Armed Services Vocational Aptitude Battery (ASVAB), a multiple-choice exam that tells the Army whether you are smart enough to be a military policeman. I am. But I'm also smart enough to be trained as an artilleryman, a water purification specialist, and a Patriot missile repairman. I don't want to do these jobs. No one else does, either. But the recruiter tells me that there aren't enough slots for the military police and he can offer me a better choice of duty stations if I take one of the jobs no one wants. When I hesitate, he says they might still be able to arrange military police training. I just need to sign first. He'll arrange it later.

I know this isn't true. Mr. Gentry warned me about recruiters desperate to fill jobs that no one wants to take. They find a way to make you sign, then rescind promises or alter agreements, and you end up tightening screws on Patriot missiles for three years. When I get up to leave, the recruiter's supervisor steps in. He says they can offer me whatever I want; I just need to be patient. Sign the paperwork and everything will work out. I keep moving toward the door. He says, "What about the language program?"

I was never aware the Army had a language program. The recruiter tells me my ASVAB score qualifies me for the Defense Language Institute (DLI). I sit back down and we talk about the life of a military linguist. He assures me the experience would benefit my pursuit of a law enforcement career, even open doors to intelligence agencies. He convinces me to sign the papers. I enlist as an Arabic linguist.

But the recruiter doesn't tell me everything. He doesn't tell me that I still have to take the Army's Defense Language Aptitude Battery (DLAB) in order to qualify for the Arabic program. If I fail the test, I'll be forced to choose from whatever jobs the Army makes available. I've signed the papers. The Army owns me for the next five years. The recruiters know that most candidates fail to score high enough on the DLAB to qualify for Arabic. They expect the same from me. When I pass the test a week later, they seem disappointed. One of them laughs and says, "Everyone flunks out of Arabic eventually." None of them wish me luck. I board a plane in Harrisburg and fly to Fort Leonard Wood, Missouri. I spend the flight thinking I should have listened to Mr. Gentry and become an officer. I wonder what else the recruiters haven't told me.

2

———

Three miles into a six-mile run and my legs begin to burn. It's Francis. He's pushing us harder than normal this morning. We began the run in formation, four columns of twelve men each, but as the pace increases, the formation begins to fall apart. Faster runners move to the front as the slower runners fall to the back.

Sergeant First Class Francis unleashes a tirade of profanity as the slowest runners fade from view. The formation turns back to pick up stragglers, forcing faster runners to cover twice the distance. Francis makes one last push. He sings a cadence to keep us in step.

I went to the church
Where all the people pray
I took out my Claymore
And I blew them all away
Singing left right, left right, left right kill
Left right, left right, you know I will.

The formation fails again. We circle back but do not continue the run. Francis orders us into a ditch on the side of the road. We rest our feet on the edge and put our hands down into the sludge. We hold the position as long as we can. Before long, we are fighting to keep our faces out of the mud. There is more profanity from Francis.

We return to the barracks, where Francis punishes us for our performance in the morning run. He starts with the electric chair. We put our backs against the wall and bend our legs. He locks us into a crouched position that results in muscle failure of the quads, hamstrings, and calves. It hurts. We raise ten-pound rubber rifles and hold them parallel to the ground. Our legs are on fire, then our arms, too. He orders us to the ground. We lie on our stomachs and stretch our hands above our heads. We roll left, we roll right, we roll left, we roll right. We do jumping jacks. We do push-ups. We do sit-ups. When muscles fail, we lock ourselves into the front leaning rest. When we can't do that, we run in place with the rifles above our heads. Then it's back to the electric chair.

At night, we serve hour-long shifts as fireguards. The barracks are quiet. There are no drill sergeants. We wax the floors and clean the toilets. I write to Don Hackett and tell him I may have made a mistake. I wake up thinking about the electric chair.

It is late October and the leaves are changing. In the mornings, there is frost on the ground. Francis marches us out into the woods to a small cinder-block building with a smokestack in the center. We are issued gas masks and chemical suits. The masks have the stale stench of fresh rubber. We suction them onto our faces and pull the straps over the backs of our heads. The eyepieces fog up. The air inside the mask is thick and difficult to breathe. When we fail to don the masks in the appropriate manner, Francis orders us to sit in the electric chair. Sweat pours down our faces inside the masks. The masks starve us of oxygen. Pools of sweat slosh around in the bottom of the mask.

Francis approaches each of us and tests the seal on our masks before marching us into the cinder-block building. Inside, there is a smoky haze that stings the back of my neck. We turn and face a large Plexiglas window, where Francis stands with a microphone and a large smile. We hear muffled orders through our masks. When we remove the masks, we vomit, we choke, we wheeze. Long strands of mucus drain out our noses and onto the grass.

On the bayonet course we sing, "Blood, blood, blood makes the green grass grow." On the rifle range we sing, "One shot, one kill, right between the eyes!" On the heavy-weapons range we sing, "Your buddy's in your foxhole, a bullet in his head, / The medic says he's wounded, but you know that he's dead."

On Sundays we are encouraged to attend chapel. We line up outside and choose between Catholic or Protestant services. Those who choose not to worship on Sundays stay behind in the barracks and are assigned cleaning details.

I attend the Protestant service. When the chaplain says something agreeable, soldiers say, "Amen." The chaplain says we aren't loud enough. He says, "I wonder what your drill sergeants would think about that? Let's try it again." The next week I try the Catholic service. No one says, "Amen," but the priest tells us that we can't just come to chapel as an escape from the drill sergeants.

There's something about the Army that makes it difficult to go to church. During the week I am singing cadences about blood and foxholes. On Sundays, I'm being told that I'm not yelling loud enough and that I can't use the church to protect me from the Army. I decide to put my head down and get through basic training without thinking about church. I'm not sure what Don would say about this. I decide not to think about that, either.

The following week, I decide to skip church and accept whatever consequence Francis has in mind. We stand in formation while the Catholics and Protestants march off to services. When they're far enough away, Francis looks in their direction and says, "Fucking assholes," before sending us back to our bunks for extra rest.

Basic training winds down and we prepare for our follow-on assignments. We stand in the hallway outside Francis's office and wait for our orders. The first sergeant calls me into his office and laughs. "Arabic? What a waste. Torture a towelhead for me." Francis stops me in the stairwell. "Linguist? I figured. Don't fuck it up."

As part of my enlistment contract, I am required to attend the Army's airborne course at Fort Benning, Georgia. It is a three-week program designed to introduce students to the world of military parachute operations. We don a parachute, we board an airplane, we fall out of the airplane, and we try to land without hurting ourselves. The instructors spend the majority of the time making jokes in an effort to alleviate nerves. On the way to the airfield we sing cadences about dying in a parachute accident.

> He hit the ground, the sound was splat, his blood went spurting
>   high!
> His comrades then were heard to say, "A hell of a way to die."
> He lay there rolling 'round in the welter of his gore
> And he ain't gonna jump no more.

On the last day of the course, the entire class marches to the 250-foot towers where we trained earlier in the course. The Army bought the towers in 1940 after witnessing them in action at the World's Fair in New York. We were dropped from the towers in order to instill a sense of confidence in our equipment. But on the day we're scheduled to jump, we sit in bleachers in front of the towers and watch mannequins fall to their deaths. The parachutes are rigged to malfunction. One type of malfunction is called a cigarette roll. The parachute deploys but fails to open. It flutters in a straight line as the mannequin plummets to the ground. The mannequins make terrible sounds when they hit the ground. Overhead, a plane flies by with a jumper in tow. The static line is rigged so it fails to release, and the mannequin flaps in the wind behind the plane. We laugh. The instructors wish us luck.

I jump out of the plane and I don't die. No one else does, either. But there are a variety of minor injuries. I fail to keep my chin in my chest during an exit and when the risers on my parachute deploy, they tear into my face. On the ground, I stick my finger through my cheek. The instructors send me to the medics and tell me to be back in time for graduation.

We receive our jump wings on the parade ground. Family and friends attend the graduation ceremony. The instructors place the shiny pins on our left breast pockets and then push the sharp edges up against our skin. They do this gently. After the ceremony they collect the jump wings and say, "Wait till tonight."

In the barracks, we receive our jump wings again. We stand in the hall and wait for higher-ranking soldiers. They pin the wings on our uniforms again and shove them into our chests. The pins penetrate. Then we fight our way down the hall as other soldiers grab the pins and shove them further. Some twist them. Some punch them. One soldier swings a Kevlar helmet. Everyone bleeds. Everyone laughs.

2.1

In December 1995, I begin studying Modern Standard Arabic. The Defense Language Institute (DLI), in Monterey, California, is the U.S. military's primary school for foreign-language instruction. All languages are covered, but the largest classes are in Korean and Arabic. I arrive at the reception office and hand the duty sergeant my orders. The orders say the program will last for seventy-three weeks.

New arrivals spend the first week in briefings. Officers and career soldiers get up front and chide us for having it so good. Never again, they say, will the Army see fit to station us in such a wonderful place. We don't deserve it, they tell us. We haven't been soldiers long enough. They say we should be suffering in some place like Louisiana, Kentucky, or Tennessee, just the way they did when they were young soldiers. We're confined to base for the first month. Like any other soldiers in training, we wake up, we clean, we run, we shower, we train, we run again, we clean again, and we sleep.

We master the Arabic alphabet on the first day. We learn to write the letters in script on the second. We learn to read from right to left. We learn to count, we learn the days of the week, the months, the colors, and the seasons. By the end of the first week, we are reading simple sentences.

Tests are scheduled every two weeks. Fail two in a row and you're out. Fail any combination of three and you're out. Fail to impress the instructors with your overall progress and you're out. The class consists of forty students broken up into four classrooms. I begin the course with twelve students in my classroom. At the end of week five, two students are out. By week seven, three more have joined them. Like most students, I assume my days are numbered. I survive each test by a thin margin, and I am pulled in by instructors and berated for my work ethic and study habits. One instructor in particular, an Iraqi civil engineer named Mumtaz, seems to enjoy berating us more than the others.

Mumtaz is the lead instructor. He is large and imposing. Students are afraid of him. Other teachers are, too. Occasionally Mumtaz enters a classroom unannounced to observe the other instructors. When he does, they become angrier and less patient. They scold us for mispronouncing words, and lecture us about our poor handwriting. The teachers tell Mumtaz they are working as hard as they can; the students simply aren't smart enough to keep up. We are lazy. We are dumb. None of us are going to pass the course. Eventually, Mumtaz takes over the class and lectures us some more.

After twenty-six weeks, there is a weeklong break. We've lost more than half the class. The remaining students show the most promise. We assume the vast majority of those who remain will be allowed to stay with the class through the final exams.

The pace quickens. In addition to basic language classes, we begin to study Middle Eastern history and politics. We visit our teachers in their homes and travel with them to Arabic-speaking communities in San Jose and San Francisco. Entire weeks are dedicated to immersion. We speak Arabic in class, in formation, at physical training, and in the barracks. DLI offers us a world-class education, and exposes us to the incredibly diverse and complicated Middle East.

Mumtaz spends time telling us about how he escaped the regime of Saddam Hussein. He was only a lieutenant during the war with Iran. He was forced to serve. He was never a real soldier. Just a driver. He never did any fighting. No one, he tells us, supports Saddam Hussein. All Iraqis hate him. None of them are in favor of the regime. Mumtaz says that if America had invaded Iraq during the Gulf War, the Iraqis would have taken up arms alongside them. He says that he would have gone back to Iraq and fought alongside U.S. forces. He says it's too late now. The opportunity has passed. Saddam learned his lesson. He will never do anything to antagonize the United States. America will never fight another war in the Middle East. He says, "Saddam will grow to be an old man."

Eventually, Army leadership gives us more freedom at DLI. We dress in civilian clothes in the evening and we can depart the base without requesting an official pass. On occasion, Mumtaz takes me to dinner. We go to a Lebanese restaurant in Monterey. He forces me to order in Arabic. He sees me pray before my meal. Mumtaz says he is Christian, too. He takes time to teach me about the Christian communities in Iraq. He tells me that Saddam treats Christians well. He leans in, looks away from me, and whispers. He says, "We have done well under Saddam. Saddam is a bad man, but he protects us from the Muslims."

Most of our Arab instructors at DLI are Christians. There are no women in headscarves and no calls to prayer. We study Arab history, but we don't talk about Mohammed, the Koran, or Wahhabism. We learn about the political systems in Egypt, Iraq, and Syria, but we never talk about Saudi Arabia or Kuwait. Army leadership reminds us that we are not to engage our instructors in discussions of religion. I don't know why this policy is in place. I don't know why we avoid the topic of Islam. But most of us leave DLI having learned next to nothing about Muslims.

On Sunday mornings, I attend a Presbyterian church in Carmel. The congregants are old. Many of them are transplants from the Northeast. The church has a beautiful organ and a wonderful choir. There is no clapping and no overhead projector. I attend an infant baptism and volunteer to teach Sunday school.

On base, students call DLI the Defense Love Institute. Male and female soldiers live on the same floor. We have been together for nearly a year. We are fit, stressed, and drunk. I start to drink on Saturday nights.

This is a significant departure for me. I had my first taste of alcohol a few weeks after my twenty-first birthday. It wasn't that I thought drinking was immoral; I thought of underage drinking as illegal. Presbyterians typically follow rules. So I did.

But I am a soldier now, and alcohol eases the stress from long days studying Arabic, so I view it as a tool to be used in pursuit of my calling. As Arabic gets more difficult, I use this tool more often. I start finding it difficult to feel good about going to church.

I meet another soldier. She is fit, stressed, and drunk. She is beautiful. I take her to dinner. She sneaks into my room at night and does wonderful things to me, far more than anything I experienced in the church parking lot during high school. I enjoy these things. I try not to think about what Don used to say about things that can't be undone. I feel good about spending time with this beautiful soldier. She is warm and kind. I have sex for the first time. I find it impossible to feel good about going to church.

As the language program moves into the final months, we take time to enjoy Monterey. We have survived an entire year. Only a few months remain. At this stage, none of us expect to be dropped from the course. We prepare for the Defense Language Proficiency Test (DLPT), a battery of exams that will judge our listening, reading, and speaking abilities. We must score at a certain level in each discipline in order to graduate from Monterey.

In class, the pace slows. For the first time in over a year, we have time to concentrate on things other than Arabic. After class, I take long runs along the Pacific coastline and enjoy the views of the ocean. I ride along 17 Mile Drive with the beautiful soldier and explore the walking trails of Big Sur. We hike and camp and build fires on the beaches. We visit the mansion of William Randolph Hearst and spend entire days at the Monterey Bay Aquarium. I take time to read

John Steinbeck and I walk on Cannery Row. I sleep until noon on Sundays.

My Presbyterian grandmother calls and says she is flying to San Francisco to see family. She wants me to show her Monterey. I don't want to be reminded of how I've drifted from her standards, so I tell her I'm too busy. I tell her it's too hard for her to get on base. I tell her I'll see her when I'm home. I tell her it's a bad time.

That Sunday morning I sit in the common room and watch the San Francisco 49ers on TV. I am hungover. I spent the night drinking hard cider, then moved on to Jack Daniel's. I'm drinking more hard alcohol now, thinking less and less about Don and the memory verses. The beautiful soldier is with me. We're not supposed to be having sex in the barracks, but we're far enough into the course now that leadership tends to look the other way.

I hear someone in the hallway say, "He's right down there." I hear my grandmother say, "Thank you." My grandmother stands in the common room at DLI surrounded by empty liquor bottles and hungover soldiers. She laughs. She introduces herself to the beautiful soldier.

My grandmother takes us out to lunch. She tells stories about the family and how some of the Burds moved out to California and why it's important for all of us to stay in touch. She asks the beautiful soldier about her family, and she learns things about her that I didn't know. My grandmother tells me these things, then orders me to ask other questions. She treats the beautiful soldier as though she is a part of our family.

My grandmother says nothing about the empty liquor bottles, and she says nothing about finding me hungover on a Sunday morning. She says nothing about how I tried to avoid her. Her unwillingness to judge is the very thing that condemns me. I feel exposed and embarrassed. I am guilty. But I am too immature to admit it. Instead, I blame the beautiful soldier. I tell myself I was led astray.

I stop drinking on Saturdays and I start sleeping alone again. I return to the Presbyterians in Carmel by myself, and I volunteer to help with the youth group. I visit the chaplain at DLI and volunteer to help him as well. I focus on Arabic. I excel in class. I try to be a good Presbyterian again. I try to stay away from people who aren't helping me. I try to focus on my calling.

Near the end of the course, there is a class picnic on the beach. Mumtaz pulls me aside and takes me for a walk. We speak in Arabic. We speak about Bethlehem Steel and Liberty High School. We talk about my father and his job as a teacher. We talk about Gordon College and Boston University. We talk about Sergeant First Class Francis and the beautiful soldier. We are sleeping together again. I tell him she has mentioned marriage. Mumtaz knows the soldier. He says, "Impressive." Mumtaz listens as I talk about all of these things. He asks questions. He insists on more detail. He tells me to speak more quickly. I speak in Arabic for over an hour.

Mumtaz holds this conversation with every student in the class. He pushes our limits. He forces us to show him what we've learned. We call it the interrogation. When we return from the picnic, he fails two more students.

The DLPT is a three-day ordeal. The speaking portion of the test comes first. I sit before three native speakers of Arabic. Their questions are familiar. They ask me all the same questions Mumtaz asked me on the beach. I speak quickly and with confidence. The proctors nod in approval. The listening portion of the exam is familiar as well. Mumtaz has been speaking about the topics during our meals at the Lebanese restaurant in Monterey. By the time I take the reading portion of the exam I know exactly what to expect. Mumtaz has already exposed us to the pertinent texts during classroom sessions. The test scores from our section exceed the required proficiency.

I do not report Mumtaz. To me, his behavior appears unethical. It's possible he could be dismissed from his position. And it's possible our test scores could be invalidated, forcing us to either take the test again, or roll back into another class and repeat part of the coursework.

I've come to respect Mumtaz. And I like my fellow classmates. I don't want to make life difficult for any of them. But it still feels dishonest. I'd like to think I'd have passed the DLPT even without Mumtaz's help, but I'll never know. It's the kind of thing Don warned me about. He warned me not to abandon voices of accountability; he warned me not to do things that can't be undone.

The class spends another week in Monterey packing rooms and preparing for follow-on assignments. I receive orders to report to the 101st Airborne Division in Fort Campbell, Kentucky. Before leaving, I spend time with the beautiful soldier. She asks about marriage again. I want to say yes, but I'm still blaming her for my behavior at DLI. I can't see it yet, but my pursuit of a calling has caused me to value my own path more than the lives of those around me.

I think of Monterey often. When I do, I think of the beautiful soldier. I knew even then that it was juvenile to think we'd done anything wrong. It was callous to think my journey meant more than hers. It was cruel to assign blame in place of my own guilt. I was sorry for the way I treated her at the end. In the coming years, I will do much worse to others.

2.2

In September 1997, I report to the 101st Airborne Division at Fort Campbell. This is the place the officers at DLI warned me about. After spending a week at a reception battalion completing paperwork and familiarizing myself with the division's policies, I'm assigned to D Company in the 311th Military Intelligence Battalion. There are a variety of units within the 311th, among them Low Level Voice Intercept (LLVI), a three-man team trained for infiltration and reconnaissance.

I spend my days and nights training as a member of an LLVI team in the open expanse of Fort Campbell. We train in small-unit tactics, marksmanship, land navigation, helicopter insertions, and ambushes. We conduct physical training five days a week. We run, we climb ropes, we carry logs, and we go on twelve-mile hikes with fifty pounds of gear. We say, "Hang in there." We say this a lot. In six months, I don't speak a word of Arabic.

In December 1997, I go to war for the first time, against the People's Democratic Republic of Atlantica (PDRA). This country is located in the swamps of Fort Polk, Louisiana, where the Army has established a multimillion-dollar Joint Readiness Training Center (JRTC). Weapons are outfitted with lasers and sensors in order to allow soldiers to practice shooting each other.

At JRTC, I die. I'm killed by simulated grenades, rifle fire, and aerial gunnery. The training center issues us casualty cards inside sealed envelopes. When our sensors indicate we've been hit we open the envelopes and announce our injuries to our comrades. Training officers stand nearby and judge the lifesaving efforts of other soldiers. One of my casualty cards reads, "Sucking chest wound." My team leader places a plastic bandage over my lungs leaving one side unsealed. He rolls me over so that I can breathe. The training officer says, "Good. Now he's in cardiac arrest. Do CPR." My team leader presses on my chest and pretends to breathe air into my mouth. The training officer says, "No, no, do it for real." My team leader presses his lips against mine and blows. The air is stale and disgusting. The training officer says, "Holy shit, you faggot, I was just kidding. Holy shit! It's gay LLVI." I recover from the sucking chest wound and get sent back to war.

We spend the week invading and reinvading the country of Atlantica. We also fight an insurgent group called the Cortina Liberation Front (CLF). The CLF is made up of fast-moving small-unit forces that harass troops throughout the night. They earn a reputation as cheaters. They don't wear the right uniforms, and they turn their sensors off so we can't shoot them. No one likes the CLF.

We deploy to Louisiana for weeks at a time. We return to Kentucky to train for Louisiana, then go back to Louisiana to be killed by the CLF and the PDRA. I excel as an LLVI soldier. I acquire a particular talent for land navigation. I become adept at identifying terrain features and maintaining an accurate pace count in order to calculate the distance we travel. I am proficient with a compass and a protractor. I instruct other soldiers in the difficult task of navigating at night. I am in the best shape of my life. From December 1997 through December 1999, I don't speak a word of Arabic.

During this time the LLVI team is attached to a group of Army Rangers from the division's Long Range Surveillance Detachment (LRSD). We spend the week in the field trying to stay warm and dry as we perform a series of exercises designed to teach us how to react to an ambush. On the last day of the exercise, we practice assaulting a fortified position. The Rangers shoot us with paintball rounds, leaving us black-and-blue. We pretend to be dead, but the sergeant in charge of the exercise orders us to keep going. His voice is familiar. As we move forward, a soldier from inside the bunker tosses a smoke grenade. It pops and hisses. I charge the grenade and pick it up. Smoke pulsates from the grenade and burns my hand. I yell, "Die, motherfuckers."

The sergeant stops the exercise and gathers us together to assess our performance. I know the voice now. It is Sergeant Francis from basic training. He's a platoon sergeant with the 101st. He recognizes me. He says, "Fair? You fucking failure, I thought you were going to be a linguist. What the fucking shit are you doing out here?"

In December 1999, after two years of endless LLVI training exercises, I receive new orders. I am attached to the Army's 10th Mountain Division at Fort Drum, New York, in support of their deployment as peacekeepers to Egypt's Sinai Peninsula. We serve under the Multinational Force and Observers (MFO), which enforces the agreement signed between the Egyptians and Israelis at Camp David in 1979. I deploy to the Middle East as an Arabic linguist.

In Egypt, a lieutenant colonel from the 10th Mountain Division is hosting a group of Egyptian officers. I am called in to translate. He begins by telling the history of the unit and its legendary service at the Chosin Reservoir in Korea. The unit was nearly massacred. He talks about a statue at Fort Drum erected to commemorate the event. I do not know the Arabic word for statue. He says something about how much snow falls at Fort Drum in New York. I do not know the Arabic word for snow. Then he tells a joke. The joke is about giving his wife a blow job. He says while he's hiking through the desert, she's stuck at home using the snow blower to clear out the driveway. He says he's going to owe her a snow blow job when he gets home. I still don't know how to explain snow in Arabic.

I spend six months in Egypt, most of them in Taba, a small city on the Egyptian-Israeli border on the Gulf of Aqaba. My mornings are spent translating for foreign liaisons and Egyptian officers at the Taba Hilton. In the afternoons, I walk to Israel, where the officers are fluent in a variety of languages. I ask them to come back into Egypt, to the Taba Hilton, and tell me what the Egyptian officers are saying.

I travel the Sinai Peninsula with an Egyptian army officer and mediate disputes between American troops and Egyptian civilians. When a U.S. Army fuel truck runs over a camel, I am invited into a Bedouin camp to offer payment. When U.S. soldiers are accused of stealing necklaces from a shop in Sharm el-Sheikh, I speak with the Egyptian shop owners and offer to cover the costs. When a chlorine tank on an American outpost ruptures, I visit sick Egyptians in the hospital and hand out MFO coffee mugs and sweatshirts. When a U.S. soldier is killed in a traffic accident, I cross into Israel and help process his body through customs and over the border. Egyptian officers mourn with me in their office. They hold my hand and kiss me on the cheek. My Arabic improves.

Near the end of my deployment to Egypt, I take a few days of leave and meet my father in Cairo. We visit the pyramids, the Egyptian Museum of Antiquities, and Tahrir Square. We buy train tickets to Luxor, but I become ill and can't make the trip. I spend two full days in the hotel room in Cairo vomiting and fighting a terrible fever. I make an effort to venture outside and see the sights, but the heat is too much for me. My father heads back to the States and I return to the Sinai Peninsula. I spend the next week recovering. An Army doctor prescribes an antibiotic. It is slow to work. There is some talk of sending me home early, but eventually I recover. The doctor tells me to get a full physical when I return to Fort Campbell. He says overseas illnesses such as mine have the potential to do serious long-term harm. He says they can even damage the heart. But that's rare.

When the deployment ends, I return to Fort Campbell. I return to LLVI. I go back to JRTC and get killed by the CLF again.

2.3

By July 1999, the Korean War–era barracks at Fort Campbell are beginning to deteriorate. They are old and cramped. The bathrooms don't always work. They are populated by young drunk males. I manage to survive. A few buildings away, a young soldier named Barry Winchell does not. I read about him in the newspaper.

Barry Winchell was dating a transgender woman. Other soldiers thought of him as being gay. He got into a fight. He won. Other soldiers taunted the loser for being beaten up by a gay man. A few hours later, the loser retrieved a baseball bat and beat Barry Winchell in the head. Barry Winchell died the next day.

I begin to attend a Presbyterian church in Clarksville, Tennessee, one that practices infant baptism and where the congregation never claps. At an adult Sunday school class we all wear name tags. A week after the Barry Winchell murder, the class leader talks about homosexuality. He mentions Barry Winchell. He says, "Love the sinner, not the sin." After the class, we drink coffee in the narthex. There have been crowds gathering outside the gates of Fort Campbell to protest the Army's treatment of gay soldiers. The class leader tells me that he doesn't know where these people come from. They must be part of a larger organization that promotes homosexuality "and those types of things." He says they're wasting their time. "It's not like they're going to convert any of you." Other members of the class have gathered around us and echo the leader's words.

I mention that I didn't live far from Barry Winchell. I tell them about the kind of suffering a soldier like Barry Winchell must have endured and how it must have been hard for him to feel protected.

But the leader says, "That's exactly why we can't have them mixed in with you guys in the first place." Everyone seems to agree with this.

Like Barry Winchell, one of the soldiers on my LLVI team is gay. I've curled up with him in hide sites and foxholes in order to keep warm. After a week of long-range foot patrols, we were tired, filthy, and disgusting. Thoughts or fears of intimacy were the farthest thing from my mind. I don't understand why that soldier felt he needed to kill Barry Winchell. But I do know the Presbyterian leader in Clarksville reminds me of the attitude that brought me so much pain as a boy, and it reminds me of the students at Gordon College who told me my family wasn't saved, and the students who compared homosexuals to murderers. It is judgmental and exclusive. It is dangerous. I stop attending the Presbyterian church in Clarksville.

2.4

In January 2000, in the Gulf of Aden, a group of men associated with Al-Qaeda load a little boat with explosives. They load too many. Their little boat sinks. Their target, the Navy's U.S.S. *The Sullivans*, is unharmed. Our first sergeant says if the men in the little boat had succeeded, we'd be going to war.

As an Arabic linguist, I'm familiar with Al-Qaeda. I know who Osama bin Laden is. I know about Ayman al-Zawahiri. But most of us think the organization is incompetent and amateurish. We know it is capable of car bombings and kidnappings, and we know it was probably involved in the 1993 World Trade Center bombing, but organizing a successful attack on a U.S. warship seems out of its league. Al-Qaeda seems like the kind of organization that would load too many explosives and sink its own boat.

At this time, there are a number of threatening organizations in the world that speak at least some Arabic, from Hezbollah in Lebanon to the Muslim Brotherhood in Egypt. Even portions of the Taliban in Afghanistan speak Arabic. And then there's always Iraq. But in early 2000, they all seem either well contained or simply not worth the trouble. It doesn't seem that bombings and terrorist attacks will lead us to war. We may rely on airstrikes from time to time, but it's not as if we're going to conduct a full-scale invasion. No one needs the Army. I don't pray for war, but I'm bored. Life in the Army is dull and monotonous. I'm tired of playing war games in Louisiana. I'm tired of living in the barracks. It's time to move on.

As I near the end of my five-year contract, my commander encourages me to consider reenlistment. I tell him about my desire to become a police officer and the possibility of a career in the ministry. He laughs. He says, "Fair, you're a soldier, a good one, don't get fucking religious on me." He encourages me to transfer to a more specialized unit called the tactical support team. He says the mission is classified. He can't tell me much about it. I think he says this to make it sound more interesting. It will require another five-year contract. It includes a $15,000 reenlistment bonus. He enrolls me in a prisoner-of-war training program. He says, "This will give you a taste of the kind of thing you'll get to do."

In early 2000, I report to the prisoner-of-war training program. It's the Army's Survival, Evasion, Resistance and Escape program (SERE), designed for soldiers in positions where there is considerable risk of capture. Each phase of the course is designed to simulate the plight of soldiers caught behind enemy lines. Our first goal is to survive on limited resources. The trainers teach us how to build traps and snares to catch wildlife. But when it comes time to learn how to prepare food in the wild, no one has captured any wildlife.

The trainers buy white rabbits from a local pet store. Each student is taught how to kill the pet rabbit. The rabbit should be relaxed when it dies in order to prevent the meat from toughening up. One of the students on my team kneels down and rests the rabbit on his leg. He pets it to keep it calm before striking it on the head with his fist. He misses. The rabbit isn't relaxed anymore. He swings again, but lands only a glancing blow. One of the officers takes the rabbit from him and slams it up against a tree. He says, "Now it's dead." He skins it. He stretches the skin from the back and cuts it open with a knife. There is a scream. It is pitiful and terrifying. We are terrified. The rabbit is screaming. He throws it to the ground and stomps and stomps until the head pops and a squirt of blood stains the grass. Someone says, "Holy shit, it's Barry Winchell the rabbit!" Everyone on the team laughs. I do, too. I'll need to drink heavily to forget about that.

The final phase of SERE school requires students to evade capture. We crawl through the woods and build hide sites. An observer from the school travels with us. When we've evaded capture long enough, he radios in our position. Simulated enemy troops arrive and force us to surrender. Once captured, we are taken to a detention facility. The trainers pretend to be enemy interrogators. They have our personnel files. They know everything about us. They threaten our families by name. At night, they play loud music. One of the guards brings in a recording of his infant son crying at night. He plays it over and over. He also plays the opening portion of Ozzy Osbourne's "Crazy Train." We strip naked and stand out in the cold. Army doctors take our pulse. During interrogation, we are promised warm meals and warm beds if we cooperate. We get slapped and shoved. They say everyone breaks down under duress. They tell us torture works. It always has. It always will. It just takes time.

In the 1990s, the Army, like the rest of the federal government, was getting smaller. Even so, it was a struggle to maintain suitable numbers of midlevel sergeants. The Army pushed hard to retain soldiers nearing the end of their first contract, because it cost too much to train replacements. They were offered lucrative reenlistment bonuses and granted requests for special postings. There were mandatory briefings about reenlistment options.

In the summer of 2000, I attend a mandatory reenlistment briefing at Fort Campbell. The sergeant major gives a PowerPoint presentation. He shows us a video: soldiers jump out of airplanes and conduct urban combat operations. Lee Greenwood sings "God Bless the USA." Bonnie Tyler sings "Holding Out for a Hero." Most of the footage is from 101st training missions at JRTC.

There are also graphs and charts and statistics. PowerPoint says that a significant majority of soldiers who return to civilian life do not find jobs that pay enough to support their standard of living. I make $18,000 a year. The sergeant major shows us a chart that adds in housing, food, uniform allowances, professional development, and a column labeled "miscellaneous." The chart says someone with my rank and experience makes the equivalent of $75,000 a year. The sergeant major tells all of us that we'll never match our salaries in the civilian world. He also shows us evidence that our educational benefits will not enable us to afford college. He laughs and says, "None of you are college material, anyway." When I was a civilian, the Army told me I needed military experience to succeed in the civilian world. Now that I'm a soldier, the Army tells me my military experience will make that all but impossible.

2.5

In September 2000, I am honorably discharged from the Army. I return home to Bethlehem. In October, in the Gulf of Aden, men load a medium-sized boat full of explosives. This one doesn't sink. It explodes and tears a hole in the Navy's U.S.S. *Cole,* killing seventeen U.S. sailors. Al-Qaeda is getting better.

I go back to the First Presbyterian Church, where my friends have spent the last five years becoming teachers, doctors, architects, and engineers. They have cars and houses and 401ks. The law-enforcement recruiters from a job fair at Fort Campbell talk about hiring freezes and budget cuts. They say, "Be patient, things will pick up soon."

Don is no longer the youth pastor at First Presbyterian in Bethlehem. He has taken another position, at a Presbyterian church in Lancaster, Pennsylvania. Lancaster isn't far, but there's no direct route. You have to drive through towns like Reading and travel on roads like 222 that go from being highways to residential streets in a matter of miles. It's an awkward drive. Or at least this is what I say to Don when I apologize for not visiting.

I take a job as a security guard at KidsPeace. KidsPeace is a kids' prison. It houses kids who can't live with other kids. The kids have been abused or raped or abandoned. There are buildings for sexual trauma, physical trauma, and substance abuse where the kids are locked inside. I patrol the grounds to make sure they don't escape. When the kids attack staff, I arrive on scene and hold the kids down. I wear khaki pants and a white polo shirt with "KidsPeace" embroidered over the graphic of a kid's handprint.

At Christmas I reconnect with an old friend from Liberty High School. Karin Sawyers is a chemical engineer with a car, a house, a 401k, and runner's legs. She attended church as a kid, but doesn't go as frequently as she once did. She wants to find a way to get back. So on Sundays we attend the early service at First Presbyterian in Bethlehem.

First Presbyterian offers a contemporary worship service now; it takes place in the church gym, where a praise band belts out songs with drums and guitars. But the early service is still held in the sanctuary, with hymns and an organ. The pastor still wears a robe and stole, and the congregants wear suits and ties and dresses. Like me, Karin is more comfortable at this service. We sit next to my grandmother, who asks Karin questions about her family and learns things about her that I didn't know. After church, my grandmother pulls me aside and tells me how much she likes Karin. And she says, "I'm so happy she comes to church."

The kind, handsome pastor from my youth is retired now. The new senior pastor is known as a good preacher, but he doesn't walk through the pews and greet us by name. My grandmother doesn't say much about him. She would never admit to it, but I know this means she doesn't like him.

The new senior pastor preaches a sermon designed to address the issue of how the Presbyterian Church should respond to the issue of homosexuality. The General Assembly, the governing body of the church, is considering changes in the church's ordination standards, which would allow gay men and women to become pastors. Karin and I sit next to my grandmother and listen as the new pastor insists that First Presbyterian is a "big tent church." This means that people from all walks of life, including gays, are welcome at our church. He says that God welcomes all sinners, including gays, into his tent. But sinners—rapists, thieves, murderers, gays—must first confess and repent before being called to leadership. When he says this, there is applause in the sanctuary. It is not tepid and reserved. It is thunderous and aggressive. And instead of the church I remember, a church where someone might be made to feel ashamed for applauding, there's a sense of shame for those who don't. My grandmother, Karin, and I are the only ones in our pew who do not applaud.

On the way home, Karin says, "Does everyone in your church think of homosexuals as rapists and thieves?" Karin and I talk about a close friend from high school who is gay. I mention the murder of Barry Winchell at Fort Campbell and the things they said at the church in Clarksville. We agree that our gay friends are not rapists, thieves, or addicts. We agree that we may no longer feel welcome at First Presbyterian Church.

We both love watching minor league baseball games in Reading. We both like to run. We like to watch movies together and we like to sit in the same room together and read books. We like to take road trips to New England and we like to go to the museums in New York. Karin likes to hear about the Army. I like to hear about her time at Lehigh University. Karin and I have much in common, but I fell in love with her in the pew at First Presbyterian Church when she refused to applaud during the sermon about homosexuals and rapists.

In April 2001, Karin agrees to marry me. There are terrible days ahead of us. We will survive them because of Karin.

2.6

At KidsPeace there is an orchard. In July, the kids pick peaches and sell them at a local stand. I work the overnight shift. In the evenings, I park the security vehicle in the orchard and listen to the Philadelphia Phillies on the radio. I get a call to help restrain a kid who is acting out. It's from the sexual abuse house. I think about grabbing small arms and legs and pinning them to the ground. I don't want to do this. I feel nauseated. I hide in the orchard and ignore the calls on the radio. I work on an application for the City of Bethlehem Police Department.

In August 2001, I attend a panel interview with the City of Bethlehem. They ask me about my strengths and weaknesses, my skills and experience, and my education and training. One of the panel members says, "I wish you'd studied Spanish instead of Arabic." They ask me why I left the Army. I tell them about all the time wasted training for a war in the swamps and forests of Tennessee and Louisiana. They hire me. In September, Al-Qaeda flies planes into buildings.

The day after 9/11, I meet with our wedding coordinator. She says the chairs in the fellowship hall are old and unattractive. Slipcovers will fix this. I don't think it's worth the money. Karin does. Her mom does, too. Karin's father insists we rent a limousine to deliver us to the reception but I think that's too fancy. In the wake of 9/11, when Al-Qaeda has finally figured out how to start a war, when there is finally a reason to be a soldier and an Arabic linguist, when there are people to protect, I find myself talking about limousines and seating arrangements.

3

In January 2002, I begin a six-month training course at the police academy. We receive training on handguns and shotguns, and we talk about the proper use of force. We learn how to use handcuffs, Tasers, and extendable batons. We dress up in big red padded suits and take turns resisting arrest.

But much of the time at the academy is spent fulfilling state training requirements. The state requires that every police officer in Pennsylvania be familiar with the vehicle code. The vehicle code is thousands of pages long. It looks and reads like a phone book. State training standards require us to read significant portions of it. The windowless, wood-paneled classroom is adorned with the class photos of the students who have come before. There are pictures from the 1950s. In the pictures, the students are sitting in the same desks, their heads down, their books opened. We sit in the desks and take turns reading aloud about taillights, stop signs, and exhaust manifolds. When we fall asleep, the lead instructor at the academy, who served in the Marines, puts us in the electric chair.

At night, I fill out applications for other law-enforcement agencies. The mind-numbing monotony of the police academy has convinced me that local law enforcement may not be my calling after all. There is a war in Afghanistan. There are weapons inspectors in Iraq. I could be there, too. I could be using my Arabic.

I speak with a friend of mine from the Army about the long days at the police academy. He's heard about a new program at the CIA. They're looking for prior military with language training and security clearances. He sends me a link to the CIA employment website. I check the boxes that designate military training, foreign-language proficiency, security clearance, and experience in the Middle East. The CIA calls the next week to schedule an initial interview in Reston, Virginia.

In June 2002, I graduate from the police academy and begin a probationary period as a police officer in Bethlehem. My first assignment is a prisoner transfer from a neighboring county. We meet another police officer in the parking lot of a strip mall and take custody of a man with an arrest warrant for felony assault. The man is tall, thin, and hard. I place my hand on the back of his arm. I drop my handcuffs. The felon reaches down and picks them up for me. I continue to struggle with the handcuffs. He says, "Relax, kid, I'm not going to hurt you." My training officer gives me a poor performance review.

As I work with various training officers, I learn that there are two distinct types. The first type works hard to get me involved in a variety of calls throughout the city. They take me to traffic accidents, domestic disputes, and medical calls. They are observers and teachers and mentors. One of these training officers demonstrates an incredible amount of compassion during our calls. When we arrive on scene, we find people who are often angry and upset. They cry, or yell, or scream. He is calm and professional. He offers reassuring words that quickly defuse impossible situations. He ministers to people in what are often their most terrible hours.

But there is another kind of training officer, too. These training officers teach me things like how to avoid getting involved. They tell me it will be difficult to survive for an entire career unless I pace myself. They tell me I will learn to hate people. They show me where to hide from the public while on a shift. We park under bridges or in dark, secluded parking lots. One officer has a special place picked out in an old cemetery on the south side of Bethlehem. It overlooks the now dormant blast furnaces of the steel mill. From the grave-yard I can see the steeple of First Presbyterian Church.

There is a call to an old brownstone near the steel mill. Like many of the brownstones near the mill, it has been turned into an apartment building for low-income residents. One of the residents has failed to pay his rent, and the landlord is insisting we evict him. The landlord has all the proper paperwork from the court system. While not legally obligated to do so, he has allowed the resident back into the apartment to collect his belongings. The resident is drunk. Now he won't leave.

This is near the end of my probationary period. One of the com-passionate training officers arrives to back me up, but he sends me in alone to see what I will do. I try to say all the right things and follow all the right procedures but the resident refuses to leave. Even-tually the training officer comes in and takes over. He does a better job and convinces the man to be on his way. I escort him outside while the training officer fills out paperwork with the landlord. Out-side, the evicted drunk wanders into the street. I order him onto the sidewalk. He wanders farther into the street, forcing cars to swerve and honk. When I approach, he says he's going to the church where they'll take care of him. I say, "I don't care where the fuck you're going, get off the fucking street." He looks me over and calls me a rookie. I grab his arm. He fights back. I strike him with my extendable baton and drop my handcuffs again.

3.1

In Reston, Virginia, a woman stands up front and admires our attire. "Nice, I actually see some color today. We want people with color in their wardrobe." Another man stands up front and asks why we think it's important to conceal our identities. We raise our hands and give wrong answers. Finally, someone says, "Because what we do is illegal."

This is the right answer. Working for the CIA isn't illegal, but working in a foreign country as a spy is. I sit for my personal interview with a man who asks me how I feel about lying for a living. He says he's read my personal essay and respects how important my faith is. He asks, "Do you see a moral conflict here? Do you see a religious one?" I say, "Sometimes it's necessary to lie to evil."

I'm told to come back for further interviews and evaluation. I'll need to schedule an entire day for language testing. I tell them it will be difficult for me to get time away from the police department. He says, "Here's your first chance to practice your new skill. You'll just have to lie."

3.2

After six months of riding with training officers in Bethlehem, I'm released from my probationary period and allowed to patrol on my own. My first call is a man with chest pain and difficulty breathing. I remember the bad training officers who told me to pace myself. They told me not to be the first person to arrive on a medical call. That was a job for the guys driving the ambulance. They said, "ABC, ambulance before cop." I do not want to be this kind of officer.

I am the first to arrive. The man is sprawled on the floor. His wife is next to him. I set my medical kit down and pull out the oxygen tank. I'm nervous. I can't get the oxygen turned on. I forget which valve is which. I stick the tubes up his nose and ask him how he feels. "I don't feel the air," he says. I say, "Don't worry, it's flowing." It's a lie. He says he feels better. His wife thanks me.

My days off come in the middle of the week, so when I go back to Reston, Virginia, for interviews with the CIA I don't have to lie to the police department about being sick. But I want to impress the CIA, so I lie to my interviewers about not having lied to the police department. They say I should get used to the feeling. They ask me why I didn't choose to reenlist after 9/11. I tell them I didn't want to spend any more time deploying to war in Louisiana. One of the interviewers is a former soldier who has been to JRTC. He tells the others this is a really good answer. We both know the war in Afghanistan will be over before the Army gets a chance to do any real fighting. And if there's a war in Iraq, we think the whole thing will be fought from the air.

Back in Bethlehem, I arrest a woman for public intoxication. She is a heroin addict. I escort her to St. Luke's Hospital to detox. I handcuff her to a hospital bed while doctors and nurses feed her a charcoal-like solution designed to absorb the drugs in her system. She secretes it onto her bedsheets throughout the night. I hold her down while the nurses change her gown. She spits and spews and curses. At times she begs for mercy. At times she pleads for help. At times she threatens to kill me. At times she urges me to kill her. At times she tells me to fuck her.

The nurses inject her with a drug that induces a moment of clarity. The veil of heroin lifts, just briefly. She cries. She reads my nameplate. She says, "Officer Fair, oh God, oh God, help me." The heroin reasserts its grip. She shits herself again. This is the worst thing I have ever seen.

Police officers and federal agents from a local task force tell me about the war on drugs. They say it is a losing war, but one worth fighting. I talk to one of the agents about the woman at St. Luke's Hospital and all the terrible things that came out of her. The agent works for the Drug Enforcement Administration (DEA) and says of all the drug addicts he's dealt with, the ones addicted to heroin are the worst. He says, "Once they're hooked, there's no way to save them." He also says that much of the heroin sold in the Philadelphia area originates from the Middle East and helps fund groups like the Taliban and Al-Qaeda. It probably helped fund 9/11. I tell him about my language skills and my military experience. He says, "Come work for us, we need you."

While waiting to hear back from the DEA, one morning I respond to a break-in. A woman on the west side of Bethlehem thinks her neighbor's house has been burglarized. The neighbors are on vacation but she sees lights on upstairs. We enter the house and find open beer cans and bottles of vodka. There are kids passed out upstairs. We wake them up and drag them outside by their feet. Most of them have marijuana. They are young. Only one of them is older than eighteen. I don't need to notify his parents. I arrest him and take him back to the department for processing.

I wait for detectives to come in and take over, but they are busy today. My supervisor says, "It's time to conduct your first interrogation." I spent weeks at the police academy learning about vehicle code infractions and traffic violations. I spent a single day learning about interrogation. I remember being told it wasn't like TV. I remember being told never to ignore a suspect's rights. I remember the instructor telling us that unless we were nearing retirement, we'd "better fucking read people their rights."

I read the young man his rights. I ask him if he'd like to talk about what happened. He says no. The interrogation ends. My supervisor says, "You fucking idiot." A lawyer arrives and the young man is released. My supervisor says, "You suck at interrogation."

Later in the week, I'm dispatched to a bar where the owner has called for assistance in removing a belligerent customer. The customer has thrown up on himself. He has pissed himself. He throws beer at me. I attempt to wrestle him to the ground but he is far too strong for me. He throws punches and roundhouse kicks. He slips and falls. I shove my knee into the back of his neck, pinning his face in the vomit and piss. Other officers arrive and help me gain control. As I lead him to the squad car he spits beer-soaked vomit onto my uniform. He calls me a faggot. My patrol sergeant says, "Don't ever let someone say that to you. You'll never get respect back. "

I take him to the station. He spits on me again. He says the same thing. My supervisor says I should interrogate him. He says, "And I don't mean read him his rights." The man attacks me in the fingerprint room. His elbow strikes hard against the side of my face, disorienting me. I am off balance and vulnerable. He grabs my neck and shoves me into a filing cabinet. He tugs at my belt and drags me to the ground. I am taking a beating, but the alcohol in his system disorients him, and I find a way to recover. I create space and distance. I draw my extendable baton and strike him on the arms and legs. He doesn't follow commands. Instead, he struggles to protect himself, raising his arms above his head and flailing with his legs.

I let him out of the cell the next morning and hand him a citation for public intoxication. He apologizes for spitting. His arms are black and blue. He says, "I'm guilty." My supervisor says, "You're getting better at interrogation." I arrest the man again a month later. He doesn't struggle. He doesn't spit on me. He doesn't call me a faggot.

Karin and I still go to the First Presbyterian Church. We're uncomfortable with the position the church has taken on homosexuality, but this also means we are less concerned about what now seem like arbitrary and inconsistent rules. Still, the church is an important part of our lives. I continue to attend a weekly prayer group, and I volunteer to teach Bible study to high school students. There's an Alcoholics Anonymous group that meets on the same night as the high school Bible study. I see the man who spat on me and called me a faggot. I pretend not to recognize him.

I respond to a call about a broken window from a newly married couple who just bought a vacant house on Bonus Hill. Bonus Hill is where Bethlehem Steel executives built large beautiful homes with their excessive annual bonuses. The married couple stand outside and flag me down. The house is supposed to be unoccupied, but a lower-level window is broken out and a light is on in the kitchen. I wait for another officer. We enter the house and search all three floors. We find empty beer bottles and drug paraphernalia. In another room, we find soiled clothing and a wad of money. We hear a noise. We draw weapons. The other officer attempts to search a bedroom closet. He pulls on the doorknob but the door fights back. He holsters his weapon, motions to the door, and pulls it open with both hands. The man who is holding the other end of the door stumbles out and falls. I jam my knee into his ear and shout something offensive. He urinates on the rug.

In the squad car the man sits in the backseat and stinks. I ask for his personal information. He says, "You don't recognize me, do you?" We went to Liberty High School together. We talk about Mr. Deutsch's history class and how we all hated Mr. Wetcher. He tells me he remembers the day Mr. Wetcher escorted me out of class. While we were gone, fellow students took Mr. Wetcher's coffee cup and took turns stuffing it down their pants. I talk about the Army and he talks about Bloomsburg University. He talks about his girl-friend in high school. I sat next to her in study hall. They got married. She divorced him. He dulled it with drugs. Heroin abused him. He lost his job. He lost fifty pounds. He lost his house on Bonus Hill. He broke in and continued to live there because it reminded him of his wife. Someone else bought the house from the bank. I wrestled him out. Now I am taking him to jail.

I tell Karin about the man from Liberty High School. She remem-bers him, too. I tell her about shoving my knee in his face and taking him to jail. She winces, as though I've hurt someone. I did every-thing right at the house. He had no legal authority to be there. He hid from the police. He resisted arrest. He refused commands. I had every right to use force. But the look on Karin's face makes it impos-sible to feel as though I protected him.

3.3

I get a job offer from the DEA. The special agent in charge of the Philadelphia office calls me personally to congratulate me. He is excited to hire an Arabic linguist with military and law enforcement experience. He says the agency is eager to get me on board. He says, "You'll be doing some impressive things."

It is the fall of 2002. Karin and I are settling into marriage. We have created routines, developed friendships with other couples, and talked about starting a family. We both appreciate our individual expe-riences after college, and we're glad to have had the chance to live our own lives for a time. The Army was a difficult stretch for me, and there was a brief period after the Army when it was difficult to find a job. Lehigh was difficult for Karin. She has spent the last seven years working her way through the male-dominated ranks of the chemical engineering world. It was a lonely journey for her. But we're settled down now. And even though the DEA will require us to be flexible and move every few years, we agree that we're happy together, and we agree that it's nice to have those difficult years behind us.

I receive a packet from the DEA with final instructions and a class date for the training center in Quantico, Virginia. I am excited to be a special agent with the DEA. I schedule a final physical with my family doctor.

In November 2002, I take my last call as a Bethlehem police officer. It is the day before Thanksgiving. There are only fifteen minutes remaining in the shift. I park my squad car in a secluded lot in the city and wait for the day to end. I curse the dispatcher when she calls my badge number. I'm sent to a northern section of the city to retrieve a runaway.

The boy is hiding across the street. He won't come home. I go across the street and tell the boy it's time to go home. The boy's friend says this isn't fair. The friend says the boy's father is abusive. The family that is sheltering the boy tells me there is "definitely something going on over there." They say the boy once spent time at KidsPeace. But the father has legal custody, so there's nothing I can do. I want to get home, and I want to start thinking about working for the DEA. The boy is in the way, so I grab him by the arm, tell him it's time to go, and escort him across the street. When I return him to his father, he cries.

3.4

The day after Thanksgiving, my family doctor calls with results from my DEA physical. The doctor says, "Are you sure you don't feel sick?"

A week later, a team of nurses is staring up at an image of my heart. One of them says, "I've never seen that before." Then she tells another nurse to call some student nurses into the room. She says, "You only get to see a few of these during your career." A catheter is inserted into my femoral artery. A wire is inserted into my neck. A real-time image of my chest cavity appears on the X-ray screen. I can see the wires enter my groin and neck and snake into my heart. The team of doctors and nurses ooh and ah at my enlarged and leaking heart. The surgeon talks to the nurses. He says, "Do you see that, right there, right there, wow. I've not seen that before. Take a good look." The catheter hurts and I make this noise. The surgeon says, "The patient seems to be experiencing discomfort." One of the nurses puts something in my IV and I stop hearing their conversations.

Later, the doctor comes to my room and uses a plastic model of a heart to help me understand my condition. He takes it apart piece by piece and explains the difference between a healthy heart and mine. He hands me the purplish plastic pieces while he works to dissect the rest of the puzzle. He is kind and compassionate. He treats me the way the good training officer treated people when everything was going wrong for them.

I ask the doctor questions and he takes time to give answers. He puts the heart back together piece by piece and then offers to take it apart again if it would help. By the time I'm in my car, I remember nothing. In my hand there is a collection of medical pamphlets with pictures of old people. On one of the pamphlets I've written a list of terms.

idiopathic
viral
non-ischemic
cardiomyopathy
leaking bicuspid valve
ejection fraction 10%

severe risk terminal cardiac arrest

implantable device

heart transplant

I remember the doctor saying that my law enforcement career was likely over. I asked him what "likely" meant. He said, "You can't be a police officer anymore."

4

"God is a son of a bitch." This is what I say to Don Hackett. Don says he understands the sentiment. He says, "You're just going to need time."

I worked as a police officer for one year. I spent very little of that time interacting with Don Hackett. But now he's the first person I reach out to. He helped me start the journey toward law enforcement. I look to him to help me understand why it has ended. I look to him to help me understand what comes next. But he just keeps telling me to be patient. He just keeps telling me to take my time.

The Bethlehem Police Department ensures that I am well taken care of. I haven't taken any of my sick days, but I still don't have enough leave to cover the time I need for additional cardiac testing. My supervisor tells me not to be concerned. The department awards me time off I haven't earned.

The diagnosis is devastating. But Karin takes good care of me. Her salary as a chemical engineer is more than enough for both of us. Her company offers generous medical benefits. She has enough vacation saved to take time to drive me to Philadelphia to see another cardiologist and get a second opinion. That second opinion is the same as the first. I will never be a police officer again. Karin sits and listens to me cry. She tells me everything will be fine. She says we'll do whatever is necessary. I don't have to work. She'll take care of that. Karin protects me.

I ask the cardiologists how much time I have. They say, "It's hard to say." This is the answer cardiologists give to most of my questions. On the way out of an appointment, one of these cardiologists says, "No alcohol. This goes without saying."

After Christmas, my family doctor clears me to return to desk work. I meet with the police commissioner in his office. He tells me they were saddened by the news and that it looked like I had a promising career ahead of me. The commissioner assigns me to the records room. I sit at a desk behind a Plexiglas wall and pretend to be a police officer. The police department is working to digitize its records. There is a large machine with a sliding tray and an overhead camera. I remove staples from old reports and place the papers in the tray. There is a large square button that squeaks when you press it. There is a beep, a whine, and a small ray of light. Every time I press the squeaky button I curse God.

There is no explanation for the cardiomyopathy. The doctors talk about genetics and viruses, but they have no real answers. They say they are sorry and they understand how difficult this must be and they will answer any questions I have. But when I ask, none of them will tell me how much longer I will live.

4.1

In February 2003, I sit with the secretaries in the records room and watch a speech about chemical weapons in Iraq. Someone says, "Imagine what you'd be doing right now if you hadn't left the Army."

Don asks if I'm afraid to die.

I tell my grandmother that I'll be leaving the police department.

I tell her I'm going to take some time off. My grandmother says, "I always thought you were going to be a pastor."

My father encourages me to read through a collection of his great-great-grandfather's sermons from the late nineteenth and early twentieth centuries. The pages are well preserved, but Reverend Campbell's handwriting is difficult to decipher. My father says, "It's about time there was another pastor in the family."

Most of Reverend Campbell's sermons deal with the importance of good behavior. He mentions two particular traits more than the others: temperance and abstinence. He talks about how failing to observe these types of disciplines can turn us away from all that is good, and separate us from God. I read the sermons hoping they will rekindle the call to ministry, but in many ways they remind me that I have already drifted too far.

The cardiologists say I should keep exercising, so Karin asks me to play on her corporate softball team. It's a welcome distraction from visiting doctors and working in the records room. After the game, players gather at a bar for drinks. I listen as engineers talk about hydrogen, membranes, and fiber bundles. They complain about customers and vacation policies. Karin talks about an upcoming work trip to Russia and simulations that need to be run. Someone makes a joke about chemical engineers. He looks to me and says, "You must understand. You live with one." Then he introduces me to another employee. He says, "This is Karin's husband. He used to be a cop. Now he's going to be a pastor."

Don says to me again, "When God closes a window, he opens a door." For the first time, Don's counsel is insufficient. I don't think a door has closed. I think I was sent in the wrong direction, and I blame Don for being an unreliable guide. I can't bring myself to accuse Don, so I pretend to agree with him that it's time to change direction, but I don't. Everyone else is closing doors. I set out to open them again.

4.2

A lieutenant at the police department asks me to shuttle police cruisers to the maintenance facility. It's a generous assignment. It gets me out of the records room. On the way back to the police department, I pass the assistant chief. No one likes the assistant chief. Later, I see the assistant chief speaking to the lieutenant. The lieutenant tells me I'm not allowed to drive police cars anymore. He says the assistant chief won't allow it. He says if someone flags me down for assistance there could be a problem, because "You're not really a police officer anymore."

In March 2003, I sit in the records room and watch Shock and Awe. I'm missing another war. I speak with a police officer who serves in the National Guard. His unit has received activation orders and will likely deploy to Iraq by the end of the year. He says, "We could have used you."

At the hospital, the cardiologist strongly recommends I receive an implantable cardiac device. It will monitor my heart and administer an electrical shock to prevent a potentially fatal irregular rhythm. I ask about malfunctions and the cardiologist says, "It's hard to say." It's also hard to say whether the device will actually work. The cardiologist says the device will close the book on any sort of career that involves physical activity. I ask about reenlisting. He says no. I ask about going to Iraq as a civilian. He says, "That's asking a lot of your heart." He says it's best to avoid careers that might be physically taxing. "At least you'll be alive."

After work I visit the recruiting station on Stefko Boulevard. I ask the recruiter if I'd need a physical to reenlist. He says yes. I tell him about my heart. He says I won't be reenlisting. The recruiter checks my records and tells me that there are private firms supporting troops in Iraq who are desperate for people with my skills. He says, "I'm pretty sure they won't ask you to take a physical."

At the police department a detective enters the records room and says, "Are you the guy who speaks hieroglyphics?" He takes me to a Syrian restaurant in Allentown. The owner's son has skipped bail on assault charges. We sit at a table in the corner and order lunch. The waitress is a native Arabic speaker with a thick accent. She struggles to understand our order so I complete it in Arabic. She is excited to meet someone who speaks her language. We talk about the language school in Monterey and the Syrian teachers who served us lamb and hummus. She talks about the meals her family makes and promises to bring us something special. She says her brother usually does the cooking, but her mother has taken over for the day. I ask about her brother. She says he's in trouble so he's staying at a friend's house. When we return to the police department the detective says, "You're good at this. You should be doing this in Iraq."

I talk to Karin about working in Iraq. She's unsure. She thought I was thinking about seminary. She liked hearing the stories about the police department, especially the funny ones, but she always felt it was the stories of compassion that mattered most. "Your eyes would light up." she says. She thinks I'll make a good Presbyterian pastor.

I don't listen to Karin, and I don't listen to the voices telling me to be patient, or give it time, or consider changing course. I apply to seminary to appease these voices and silence the advice. In the meantime, I chart my own path back. I intend to make Iraq the first step.

4.3

In June 2003, in the basement of Bethlehem's city hall, I turn in my police equipment. I hand over the extendable baton, the pepper spray, and my badge.

As I look into a variety of contracting companies, I also send applications to the State Department, the Defense Department, and the National Security Agency. When I left the Army in 2000, most federal agencies were trimming their budgets and reducing their payroll. But in the wake of 9/11, opportunities within the intelligence community are endless. I make copies of my discharge record,

Airborne certificate, Arabic certification, and SERE school gradua-tion certificate. I tailor my résumé to highlight my experience in the Middle East and my language skills. In the cover letter, I write about feeling obligated to do my part.

The NSA is the first to respond. While I'm no longer proficient enough in Arabic to qualify as a linguist, my familiarity with the language will be useful in the role of an intelligence analyst. As part of the application process to the NSA, I meet with a government psychologist for personality testing and an interview. As he looks over my résumé and work history, he asks about the variety of tran-sitions I've made over the last three years. He wants to know whether I have any concerns about my stability or my decision-making abil-ities. I offer explanations for the changes. I say I'm comfortable with my decisions. I say, "Sometimes doors just get closed." He writes something down and wishes me luck.

The NSA hires me in October 2003. I move into an apartment in Glen Burnie, Maryland, while Karin stays in Bethlehem. I tell Karin and the other voices that it's only temporary, that I'll live and work in Maryland while I wait to hear back from Princeton Theological Seminary.

4.4

In Maryland, I attend an orientation class with a variety of newly hired NSA employees, among them personnel who will be working with the NSA as government contractors. Many of the contractors are recently retired NSA and CIA employees. As the NSA continues to grow in the aftermath of 9/11, it's a struggle to replace retiring employees, so they simply rehire many of them as contractors to do the same job. I sit with an older man who has worked for a variety of contracting companies throughout his career. I tell him that my primary goal is to deploy to Iraq. He asks about my background. He says he worked for a company that is looking for people like me.

He says "They'd hire you in a heartbeat." He hands me contact information for CACI International in Arlington, Virginia.

That night, from the apartment in Glen Burnie, I speak with a hiring manager from CACI looking to hire intelligence analysts who are willing to deploy to Iraq. I tell him I've only worked at the NSA for a few days. He says, "Doesn't matter, we just need your security clearance." NSA employees hold the highest-level security clearance within the intelligence community. Contracting companies don't have (or don't want to commit) the resources necessary to qualify their employees for these clearances. It is more cost-effective for contractors to poach from agencies like the NSA and CIA whose employees already have the necessary credentials. The contracting companies then assign these new employees to overseas postings that the intelligence agencies are unable to fill on their own.

The hiring manager at CACI is reading over my résumé as we speak on the phone. He says he hasn't had time to review it. He's been too busy. They've been sending people over to Iraq every week. He comes across the section on the Bethlehem Police Department. He says, "No one told me you were a cop." He reads through my military training record. He says, "No one told me you went to SERE school." He asks if I'd be willing to reapply to CACI as an interrogator. He says, "It'll be more interesting than being an intelligence analyst."

On paper, the experiences of SERE school and the Bethlehem Police Department have qualified me to do this work. In reality, I know nothing about interrogating Iraqi prisoners of war. But then, neither does anyone else. The Army does not have a significant number of interrogators with real-world experience. They have even fewer who speak Arabic. Those who do have spent their careers fighting fake wars at JRTC and interrogating role players pretending to serve in the Cortina Liberation Front. Some agencies, such as the FBI and CIA, may have experience questioning terrorism suspects, but the task of processing thousands of Arabic-speaking prisoners of war at a time is entirely different. On some level, it feels like law enforcement. And as I speak with the recruiter from CACI on the phone, I allow him to convince me that it's something I'm qualified to do.

In the meantime, I am assigned a desk at the NSA. I am sent to a variety of training classes designed to introduce me to the myriad divisions within the agency. As classes drag into the afternoon hours, most new employees struggle to stay awake. Although the NSA sends a few of its employees to Iraq, I need to complete the two-year training program in order to become eligible. I decide I cannot tolerate two years at the NSA.

4.5

By the time the hiring manager for the interrogation program at CACI calls, I've accumulated dozens of examples highlighting my relevant experience. But I never need them. The hiring manager introduces himself, tells me he was a Marine, says he hates the Army, and asks when I'll be ready to leave for Iraq.

I call a friend from my days in the Army who now works for the FBI and ask for his advice about deploying to Iraq as an interrogator. He tells me not to worry about my qualifications. He says the field interviews I conducted as a police officer are experience enough. He also tells me to be careful about contracting companies. He tells me to stick with the NSA. He says, "Go with the professionals, steer clear of the amateurs." He says, "Whatever happened to seminary?"

I receive another call from CACI. It's from a supervisor within the interrogation program. He says, "I hear you're our new interrogator."

There is no interview. There are no calls to my supervisors at the police department. There are no calls to my supervisors at the NSA. There is no medical exam. There is no background investigation. They are determined to get me to Iraq as quickly as possible. They fax me a job offer worth $120,000 a year.

My supervisor at the NSA is supportive of my decision to take the position in Iraq. He says he'd be doing the exact same thing if he were just a few years younger. I offer to give two weeks' notice, but he refuses and encourages me to go home and spend time with my family before the deployment. He shakes my hand and tells me my job will be waiting for me when I get back. As I clean my desk, other NSA employees approach and say encouraging things about the assignment I've accepted. They say, "Stay safe, wish I was going with you."

But as the country gears up for war, almost no one goes to fight it.

In December 2003, Karin and I talk about logistics. She helps me set up direct deposit. We buy a cell phone with an extra battery. We're not sure how international calls will work from Baghdad. I organize sets of clothing that can be mailed in the coming months as weather conditions change. We decide on the best digital camera to buy. I look for the one with the most storage, in the event I am unable to download the photos. I give Karin a list of numbers for the Princeton Theological Seminary. I tell her she's allowed to open the acceptance letter when it comes.

We do not talk about the police department, the ministry, my heart condition, or Iraq. And I am still too selfish to ask much about her.

4.6

At the end of 2003, my grandmother is living in Kirkland Village, a Presbyterian retirement home where the halls are decorated with yellow ribbons and patriotic balloons. Most of the doors have an American flag displayed. I visit her often in the days before my departure, hoping to hear about relatives who went off to war and the stories of their returns, but instead the conversation is awkward. My grandmother is part of a small group of residents at Kirkland Village, mostly women, who quietly question the war in Iraq. They clip articles from the *New York Times* and the *Washington Post,* then distribute them at their weekly bridge gatherings. My father and I call them the Kirkland Insurgents.

My grandmother hands me the articles one by one and says I should read them. She means it. So I sit in the century-old rocking chair and read articles about the war in Iraq while she sits and watches over me. I respond as well as I can, talking about the need to remove a terrible leader and protect the people who are suffering, but she's not impressed. She says, "Well, Eric, I just don't understand." When my grandmother says she doesn't understand, she's telling you that you're doing something wrong. She asks about seminary and says she doesn't understand why I keep finding reasons not to go.

As I prepare to leave for Iraq, Karin and I continue to talk about things like direct deposit and digital cameras. My parents talk about retirement. My sister talks about the best way to navigate new security measures at the airports. My friends talk about the Philadelphia Eagles and their nine-game winning streak.

I'm scheduled to leave for Iraq in late December. Saddam Hussein is captured on December 13. There is talk about the conflict coming to an end. Wars don't last long anymore.

5

My father drives me to the airport in Philadelphia. He says something about Vietnam and how he remembers visiting the recruiter, and he tells me that story I used to love about how the Army was going to send him to flight school and the helicopters being shot down with tennis balls. He talks about Jerry Zerfass, one of his students at Liberty High School, who was killed in Vietnam. I've heard this story before, too.

Normally, I ask my dad to tell me more about Jerry Zerfass, but not this time. I'm silent, and it's awkward, so my father talks about his newly installed EZPass. Despite heavy traffic on 476, we breeze through the tollbooths at Plymouth Meeting. He talks about how much time he saves with the EZPass. He says I should get one when I come back. We argue about what time zone Baghdad is in.

My father drops me off at the departure terminal. He offers to park and come inside, but I tell him it's best he doesn't do this. We stand on the curb and say good-bye. I say to my father, "I'm tempted to just call this off." He says, "That's probably a good idea." Then he opens the car door and says, "Let's go home." I say, "I'll call you when I get there."

From Philadelphia, I fly to El Paso. I have paperwork from CACI instructing me to report to Fort Bliss, where CACI personnel will assist in my predeployment processing. At the airport there are signs directing Department of Defense civilians to check in at the Fort Bliss in-processing desk. The desk has a series of clocks that display current times in a variety of cities around the world. It is six p.m. in Baghdad. My father was right. I stand in line with other civilians and wait for an Army sergeant to tell me what to do. The Army sergeant says they can't keep track of everyone who's coming and going, so it's best to just get on the bus and hope for the best at Fort Bliss. I can't find the CACI representative and I don't want to leave for Fort Bliss before checking in, so I let the bus go without me. By the time the next bus is available, four hours later, there is still no CACI representative at the airport.

Like most soldiers, I hated the Army during my time in service but eventually came to respect it as organized and efficient. Assignments and duties were well laid out. But the arrival in El Paso is different. The process is confused and disorganized. There are men in uniform, but it doesn't feel like the Army.

The bus drops me off in front of a barracks complex at the base. A few of the other civilians ask the bus driver where they're supposed to check in. They ask him which barracks they should stay in. They ask him what comes next. The bus driver doesn't know any of these things. We unload our bags from underneath the bus and stack them on the sidewalk. Other civilians pass by and say, "Better hurry, there aren't enough bunks for everyone."

The man next to me catches me rolling my eyes. We introduce ourselves and make a joke about quitting and going home. He says, "I could be home before my wife goes to sleep." I say, "Me, too." This is Michael Bagdasarov. He works for CACI. He is an interrogator. In less than five months we will return from Iraq together, both regretting having missed this first opportunity to go home to our wives.

Groups of people start grabbing their bags and heading into the barracks. Bagdasarov and I stay put and allow the crowd to thin. When it does, there is a young man sitting on his luggage looking lost. This is John Blee. He has been hired by CACI as an intelligence analyst. He likes our joke about quitting and heading home to our wives. He has one, too. She lives in Texas. He says we should just rent a car so we can drive to her parents' house, where they'd be happy to put us up for the night. It's two hours away. John Blee will quit Iraq before Bagdasarov and I do. He'll take a job at Guantánamo Bay.

The three of us are alone. From the sidewalk we watch the other civilians traipse in and out of the numerous buildings within the complex, carrying their gear and looking for bunks. Blee says we should hurry and find a spot before they're all gone. Bagdasarov and I tell him to wait. The group thins as it makes its way from building to building. When the group is done fighting for rooms, we carry our gear and find bunks in one of the buildings they never explored.

In the morning we follow the crowds outside and make our way to an auditorium, where an Army sergeant gives a daily briefing. He tells us that as new arrivals we are required to report to a building where the Army will begin our in-processing. Bagdasarov asks the sergeant about CACI and where we might find our representatives. The sergeant says, "Never heard of them." At the in-processing building we struggle to fill out paperwork. We say things like "I still don't understand which block I'm supposed to fill in." There is an Army corporal in charge and he tells us to check with our company representative. We tell him we work for CACI. He laughs. He says, "Oh, right, her, she only works on Thursdays."

On Thursday, after two full days in the barracks, we meet Michelle Fields. Michelle looks younger than Blee. She was hired three weeks ago. She has never worked for CACI in the past and she has never been to their headquarters in Virginia. She works in town as a dental assistant. She has no answers. We ask her how to fill out the empty spaces on the questionnaires. She says, "I was hoping you could tell me." She hands us black tote bags that say "CACI." Inside there are T-shirts, mouse pads, and a travel mug that says, "CACI, Ever Vigilant." The three of us make more jokes about going home. Randy Kutcher and Mike Henson enter the room. Kutcher and Henson are the most recent CACI hires. They served in the Marines. They decline the tote bags. They make fun of us for accepting ours.

Kutcher and Henson know each other from their time in the Marine Corps. While they never served in military intelligence, they did work in positions that required low-level security clearances. Kutcher, the taller and older of the two, guarded the Navy's supply of nuclear weapons. Henson, whose goatee matches Kutcher's, is in his midtwenties, barely older than Blee. He served as a helicopter mechanic. Helicopters have sensitive equipment. Mechanics are issued security clearances. Both men have long hair. They are adorned with tattoos. They wear hats with iron crosses. Blee says, "How in the hell did these guys get security clearances?"

Later we learn that most of the hiring managers at CACI are Marines. Marines view themselves as a cut above all other military branches. They take care of each other. The Marine hiring manager was tasked with finding individuals with security clearances to work as intelligence analysts in Iraq. Like all hiring managers working for recruiters, he struggled to locate qualified candidates. Like some hiring managers, he got creative. He recruited other Marines with lower-level security clearances, like Kutcher and Henson. Then he convinced the government that these lower-level security clearances would allow contractors to complete basic tasks until a higher-level clearance could be obtained. He also got creative with job descriptions. Kutcher and Henson were not intelligence analysts, but the recruiter molded their experience to make it sound as if they were.

After the meeting with Michelle Fields, the five of us return to the barracks. Blee's suitcase and duffel bag have been thrown out into the stairwell. Bagdasarov and I find our belongings scattered in the hallway, as well. A group of young men from a company called Blackwater has commandeered the wing where we were staying and moved out everyone else's personal belongings. Blee says something to one of the Blackwater employees. The Blackwater employee tells Blee to go fuck himself. Kutcher and Henson happen to be close by. They stand alongside Blee. They dare the Blackwater employee to say something else to Blee. He doesn't. Eventually, we gather our gear and look for new bunks. Kutcher and Henson are there to help us.

We find a group of bunks in a secluded corner of the barracks. Then all five of us clear out the belongings of other civilians and leave them in the hallway. When these employees confront us, Kutcher and Henson are there to tell them to go fuck themselves.

The second day at Fort Bliss, Michelle Fields is nowhere to be found. She doesn't answer her phone and she doesn't respond to emails. Without the help of anyone from CACI, the five of us manage to navigate the initial stages of the deployment process over the next few days. The Army assigns us an in-processing number that allows us to schedule appointments with a variety of administrative offices on Fort Bliss. We find that we are required to have dental X-rays, medical paperwork, powers of attorney, and immunization records. None of us have this information. The soldiers in charge of processing wave us through and tell us to get these things once we're in Iraq. Bagdasarov asks the soldier how we're supposed to get these things in Iraq. The soldier says, "Iraq has dentists and lawyers."

The Army requires all civilian contractors to get the smallpox vaccine. The disclaimer for the vaccine is full of dire warnings about preexisting medical conditions. There is a special section warning patients with cardiomyopathies to avoid the vaccine. I tell the doctor administering the shots that I have a cardiomyopathy. He asks questions about my condition. I give honest answers. He says I shouldn't be deploying to Iraq. I tell him my doctor has given me full clearance. He asks for proof. I don't have it. He says, "Do you want to go to Iraq or not?" After that, I get in line with Blee for anthrax.

On our third day at Fort Bliss, I stand in a line to meet with an Army lawyer who will help to prepare my last will and testament. There is a group of employees from KBR, one of the largest contracting companies in the country. They have been hired to provide logistical support to Army supply units throughout Iraq. Most have managed warehouses or distribution centers in the United States. We ask one another about pay, benefits, and vacation policies. We all complain about our employers and how uninformed we are about the process to get into Iraq. We pump one another for information, sharing rumors we've heard from other contractors and the unofficial musings of soldiers who know someone who has already deployed.

At night, the five of us sit in the barracks and complain about CACI. Kutcher and Henson talk about the bonuses they were awarded for agreeing to deploy before January 1. Bagdasarov, Blee, and I were never offered this money. Kutcher gives us the name of the hiring manager who awarded him the bonus and tells us to call the manager and act as if it was offered to us as well. Blee says this is wrong. He says we should stick to the contract we signed. Kutcher says, "Take what you can." Bagdasarov and I talk Blee into asking for the bonus. We call the manager and lie about the contract. CACI agrees to award each of us an additional $2,500.

While Blee is on the phone, Kutcher and Henson raid his suitcase. When he gets back, we ridicule him for adhering to the official CACI packing list. He has the right number of socks, underpants, and disposable razors. He has individual packets of baby wipes stored in a ziplock bag. Henson holds him back while Kutcher inventories every last item. He comes across Blee's Bible. They don't make fun of him for this.

Eventually, I tell the group about my plans to attend seminary when I get back from Iraq. Kutcher says, "And we thought Blee was the Jesus freak." They start calling me the pastor. At night, when we complain about CACI, they keep track of my profanity. There is a running tally of the number of times the pastor says "fuck." Apparently, when talking about CACI, I say "fuck" a lot.

After five days at Fort Bliss, everyone is anxious to leave for Iraq. The last day of processing is spent at the base supply unit, where we are issued our equipment. Every civilian employee, regardless of company or job title, has been promised body armor. Some, including CACI employees, have been promised weapons. At supply, we receive neither. It's a Thursday, so Michelle Fields is in her office. She assures us the equipment will be waiting for us once we arrive at a staging base in Kuwait. We get angry and tell her this is not what we were told during our phone interviews. Bagdasarov is incensed. He demands answers. Michelle promises to make a phone call and clear things up. She tells us we will have all our questions answered by the CACI representative in Kuwait. She leaves. We never see her again. In the meantime, we draw clothing, sleeping bags, canteens, and gas masks.

That night I call Karin. I tell her about Kutcher, Henson, Bagdasarov, and Blee. I complain about Michelle Fields. I tell her about smallpox. I tell her about the gas mask. I ask her whether we've received anything from Princeton. She tells me about dinner at my parents'. She complains about a neighbor who didn't shovel his sidewalk properly. She describes a doctor's appointment. The conversation is stale and tired. We say goodnight. Blee and Bagdasarov are finishing up phone conversations with their wives, too. Blee is crying.

After a week at Fort Bliss, I've met four men who will be working with me in Iraq. Two are qualified to do their job; three of us, including me, are not. Our liaison from CACI avoids us. A number of promises have already been broken. We're surrounded by other contractors who know less about what to expect in Iraq than we do. The Army seems unconcerned with our qualifications or experience. They overlook gaps in our paperwork and make exceptions to rules whenever convenient.

On the way back from an appointment at the financial office, I overhear another contractor talking on a cell phone. He's talking to a high school football coach in Georgia. He talks about his playing days at a junior college in Florida. He mentions a mutual friend and then thanks the coach for offering him a position on the staff. He'll be available for the winter weightlifting sessions and spring practices. He just needs to spend a few weeks in southwest Asia. When he hangs up the phone, he talks to another contractor. He tells the other contractor he is going to spend one day in Iraq to earn a $10,000 bonus before resigning and returning home to coach football. He offers to put the other contractor in touch with his hiring manager. He says, "It's easy money, take what you can."

I think about what my friend from the FBI said about sticking with the professionals, what he said about not trusting contractors.

I think about going home. But I also think about what the psychologist from the NSA said during the hiring process. He said my frequent career changes demonstrated instability. I don't want to look unstable. More important, I don't want to look like a coward.

I want to go to Iraq because I feel obligated to do my part, obligated to serve alongside my colleagues, and obligated to contribute to a national war effort. But I also want to go because of the way it makes other people think about me. Heart failure closed a door. Iraq will open it.

The experience at Fort Bliss makes it clear that CACI and other contractors are not properly prepared to send their employees overseas. At best, they are disorganized. At worst, they are indifferent. But there is an expectation that things will improve once we make the transition into Iraq. It is December 2003. Little is known about the impact contractors will have on the war in Iraq. Most Americans know nothing about CACI, KBR, or Blackwater. Even fewer know anything about places like Fallujah, Mosul, or Tikrit. And no one has heard of Abu Ghraib. In 2003, working in Iraq as a contract interrogator still sounds like a path back to law enforcement. I have doubts about CACI, but they're overshadowed by my desire to find my purpose again. My purpose was to protect people, but I've lost sight of that focus. I'm going to Iraq to protect myself.

5.1

After ten days at Fort Bliss, the Army transports us to an airfield where we board a chartered civilian aircraft for the flight to Kuwait. I sit next to a civilian who is wearing a shirt and tie. He is a Blackwater employee. I tell him about having my luggage moved out of the barracks by his comrades. He says, "That was the younger crew, shitbags, bottom-of-the-barrel types." He asks about CACI. We talk about DLI, Egypt, the 101st, and SERE school. We talk about the police department and my experience with weapons. We talk about seminary. He offers me a job. He says, "Not with the bottom-of-the-barrel types. And we'll give you all the weapons you want."

The CACI representative is not there to greet us when we land in Kuwait. Instead, we find other CACI employees who are expecting to meet the CACI representative on our plane. We ask them about body armor and weapons. They laugh. One of them says, "You've been talking to Michelle Fields, haven't you?" The Army instructs us to put our names on a flight manifest and wait until a military transport becomes available into Iraq. We ask about CACI. No one has heard of the company.

We rest in large circus tents near the airfield and wait for news on a flight into Baghdad. There is a large-screen television near the front. We watch *Saving Private Ryan* and *Full Metal Jacket*. On Sunday morning, I walk to a tent where a chapel service is being held. On the way, I meet the Blackwater employee from Fort Bliss who offered me a job during the flight. He's wearing body armor and carrying weapons. I tell him I hope to get my body armor and weapons in Baghdad. He reiterates the job offer, so I skip chapel and have breakfast with him. I tell him if things don't start improving with CACI I'll give him a call.

I spend five days in Kuwait. It has taken me nearly two weeks to go to war. I have no body armor. I have no weapon. I have a job offer from Blackwater. On the morning of my flight to Baghdad I check email at the Internet café. There is a message from Karin. I've been rejected by Princeton Theological Seminary. I am relieved.

5.2

"No, there's no body armor, but we'll have it soon." This is what the CACI representative tells us in Baghdad. It is the first time we have met someone from CACI since Michelle Fields abandoned us with the gas masks in Texas. There are no weapons, either. The representative will get back to us on that one.

CACI personnel in Baghdad are housed on Camp Victory, the

expansive U.S. military base near Baghdad International Airport. They have secured a series of small buildings and established living quarters for the two dozen employees currently in Iraq. The complex is affectionately called CACIville. New arrivals are assigned a room within it and issued a case of bottled water. Bagdasarov, Blee, Kutcher, Henson, and I stick together and occupy the same room. Inside, we sit on canvas Army cots and wait for instructions. We cough and wheeze as our lungs adjust to the dust-filled air of Iraq. Like every other foreigner arriving in Iraq, we are stricken with sore throats and fevers. Kutcher and Henson make fun of Blee. Everyone continues to keep track of my profanity. I don't tell anyone about the rejection letter from Princeton.

Bagdasarov, Blee, Henson, and Kutcher are assigned positions at a large prison complex fifteen miles west of Baghdad. CACI employees call it Abu G. No one wants this assignment. There are rumors about bad food and crowded sleeping quarters. CACIville is far more desirable: we are near the Bob Hope Dining Facility, well known for serving steak and lobster on Friday nights. It's where President Bush served Thanksgiving dinner to the troops in 2003. We are near the airport, where the duty-free sells alcohol. We are near clean showers and operating toilets provided by KBR. There is a base store nearby that sells Doritos and Gatorade.

I receive an assignment in Baghdad. My contract calls me an interrogator, but in the time it has taken CACI to process me through Fort Bliss and get me to Iraq, the company has pitched a new contract to the government. CACI will provide the military with HUMINT support teams (HST). These teams are designed to develop relationships with Iraqis and gather intelligence from a number of sources throughout the region. Members of these teams are required to have language abilities and high-level security clearances. There are only a handful of interrogators working for CACI who speak Arabic, and none of them hold a security clearance as high as mine. For now, I'm the only one qualified to work in this position. I'm told to sit tight and wait for other employees like me to arrive. I ask how long. "Three or four days, a week at most."

The five of us spend one final day at CACIville. We drive to Baghdad International Airport. There are no passengers or flights, but the duty-free shop is open. We wander through the abandoned airport. We climb the escalators that are frozen in time. We pass by the empty booths at passport control and we walk past the darkened storefronts and food courts. The tarmac is crowded with dormant aircraft painted in the lime-green color scheme of Iraqi Airways. I buy Jack Daniel's and Jim Beam.

On Camp Victory, we receive incoming mortar fire, but the immensity of the base makes it ineffective. We sit on the roof of our building, drink whiskey, and listen to the mortars land in empty fields. A CACI employee who has been to Abu Ghraib sits with us and says, "Just you wait."

The next morning CACI leaders organize a convoy to transport the new hires who have already been assigned to work at Abu Ghraib. The onsite CACI manager says I should consider going to Abu Ghraib as well. He says I can come back to Camp Victory as soon as my other teammates for the HST arrive. "It will be good experience for you." He says I'll only be gone a week or two. He says, "If you go to Abu Ghraib, we can give you body armor." Kutcher convinces me to go along. He doesn't trust CACI. He says the five of us should stick together.

I attend the convoy brief, where, at last, I am issued body armor. It belonged to another CACI employee who quit earlier in the morning. We're told he was the kind of person who just wasn't cut out for this type of work. A CACI supervisor says, "This isn't for everyone. You have to be the type of person who wants this." CACI confiscated the employee's body armor and sent him to the airfield in Baghdad to wait for a flight. The airfield was mortared while he waited. His blood type is written on the front of the body armor. I cross it out and write "O positive." There are still no weapons.

There is an Army liaison at the convoy brief. He has been instructed to assign a soldier to each of our vehicles to serve as protection during the convoy. Our vehicles are white Toyota Land Cruisers. CACI leased them from a company in Kuwait. The lease requires that the vehicles be returned in their original condition, so CACI does not allow us to alter the vehicles. They have no radios, no first-aid kits, and no armor. The Army liaison inspects our vehicles and decides not to assign soldiers to them. He calls them death traps. He says, "Not one of my guys, no fucking way."

CACI leadership decides it's best to opt out of the Army convoy and send us to Abu Ghraib on our own. We'll have a better chance of just blending in with other Iraqi drivers. It's early January 2004. The impression is that there is no war in Iraq, just some remaining pockets of resistance. Still, bad decisions seem to keep piling up. Though we're no longer in uniform, we still think of ourselves as part of the military operation. But now the military wants no part of us. Asking us to drive the streets of Iraq on our own without weapons, radios, or first-aid kits is a recipe for disaster. But I don't want to be the type of employee who can't handle this sort of thing. I don't want to be the kind of person who isn't doing his part. This may not be for everyone, but I want it to be for me.

The one CACI employee among us who has been to Abu Ghraib drives the first vehicle. He tells us to keep up; then he distributes foreign-made machine guns. He says U.S. soldiers confiscate these weapons during searches and raids on the streets of Iraq. He tells us we're not allowed to have weapons, but that "no one in their right mind drives to Abu Ghraib without a weapon." He doesn't tell us how he acquired the weapons. No one asks. Kutcher shows us how to operate the safety on an AK-47. He commandeers a vehicle and assigns us seats.

We depart Camp Victory and head out to the main highway. A large group of Iraqi pedestrians crowd the on-ramp in an effort to slow us down and sell us Coca-Cola. We drive over the curb and weave our way past the crowd. As we make our way back onto the road, a group of children throw rocks at the vehicles. We roll up the windows.

It is a thirty-minute drive to Abu Ghraib from Camp Victory. Halfway there, we encounter an Army convoy idling on the side of the road. We are directed to the command vehicle, where we find the Army liaison who wouldn't let his soldiers ride in our vehicles. He says there is something on the road up ahead. They are waiting for an ordnance-disposal team to come and clear the route. The liaison says to just seek cover in our vehicles and wait it out. We remind him our vehicles have no armor. He says, "Good luck."

There is an argument about what to do. The Land Cruiser with the CACI employee who has been to Abu Ghraib pulls onto the road and departs. We stop arguing and follow him. The soldiers at the front of the convoy sit in the safety of their armored vehicles and wave us through.

We arrive at the prison without further incident. As we pass through the front gate, we store the foreign weapons under the seats. We follow the lead vehicle to a prison building with a large mural of Saddam Hussein wearing a fedora and waving a rifle above his head. The CACI supervisor who has accompanied us on the trip gathers us together and makes brief introductions. Henson and I consolidate our bags while the others scout out living arrangements. Three CACI personnel return to the vehicles and prepare to head back to Baghdad. One says, "No way I'm spending the night here."

Abu Ghraib prison is an extensive network of concrete and cinder-block buildings separated by large empty expanses of dirt and mud. A matrix of walls and enclosed compounds limits the field of view, making it difficult to perceive just how large the prison is. The addition of concertina wire, HESCO barriers, and enormous piles of sandbags creates a dusty labyrinth with myriad openings into large undefined spaces. The complex, like every other part of Iraq I've seen, is flat. There is almost no vegetation. There are no views or overlooks. All you see is prison.

The site manager at Abu Ghraib assigns us bunks inside one of the many empty prison cells. We are cramped but glad to be together. Outside our room, near the head of the hallway, there is a whiteboard with messages for personnel working at the prison.

The Following is available at Supply : (Milatary Personel)

Brow T Shirts	Size XL, XLL
Brown Briefs	Size 32, 34, 38, 40
Black Socks	Size L, XL

*Interceptor Vest Plates are available for MEDIUM vest ONLY

MORTAR WARNING
Possible attack 2200 and 2300 hours tonight
Stay inside

I take a photo of the board and send it home in an email. I write something about the spelling mistakes.

We spend our first night at Abu Ghraib getting oriented to the prison. We follow other employees to an old cafeteria, where CACI personnel brief us on our assignments. Local workers have been painting over the murals of Saddam Hussein in this room. They must not have had a stepladder. The paint only covers the lower portion of the mural, leaving Saddam's head untouched. His head stares down at us as we squeeze into concrete benches and dining tables where Iraqi prisoners once ate their meals. There is a television in the corner, where soldiers are watching the Baltimore Ravens. They're asked to turn down the volume for our meeting.

There is a thump. Then more. Everyone scatters. There are more sounds. They are deep pounding noises, like someone slamming a door. These are mortars. Up above, something growls. These are rockets. They overshoot and detonate somewhere else. The CACI employee who said, "Just you wait," now says, "I told you so."

The briefing continues. CACI personnel tell us not to get too comfortable in our cells. They tell us we'll be moving a lot and to just get used to it. They tell those who have body armor to wear it in the chow hall. They assure the ones who don't have armor that it will be arriving soon. Be patient. They say the towelheads have every building in the complex ranged. They say no more hot meals for dinner. They say be prepared to have MREs for lunch. They say not to throw shit paper in the portable toilets. It takes up too much space and there is no telling when anyone will come to suck out the shit. They tell us no more showers. There's just not enough water right now. They tell us to stay off the roof. The snipers are back. They tell us to be careful about what we write in emails. They say not to take pictures of the detainees. They say, "We mean it this time." They tell us to work hard in the booth. "That's the only place where we can make any of this better."

My concerns are growing. The transition from Kuwait, to Baghdad, to Abu Ghraib was disorganized and unprofessional. It was also dangerous and irresponsible. As former soldiers and Marines, none of us were comfortable with the lack of planning, lack of support, and lack of proper supplies. No weapons, no communications equipment, no maps, and nothing for first aid. We all expect something to go wrong very soon.

But the longer each of us stays, the more tolerant we become. What seemed unreasonable at Fort Bliss seems acceptable in Iraq. All of us talk about quitting, but no one wants to be the first to do it.

5.3

In the morning, we are taken to the Interrogation Control Element (ICE). The ICE is a plywood structure adjacent to what soldiers call the hard site, the facility where the Army holds high-value prisoners. Throughout the complex there are auditoriums, cafeterias, offices, meeting rooms, and cells where Iraqi prisoners and guards worked and lived during the days of Saddam. There is ample space, but Army engineers are unsure about the buildings' structural integrity. They're not sure how they will stand up to the mortar fire and rocket fire. They're afraid the buildings may collapse if hit too many times, so they build temporary plywood structures instead.

The interrogation booths are part of a small plywood structure just outside the ICE. There is a central hallway with six interrogation booths on each side. A two-way mirror runs the length of the hall-way. We walk down the hallway and observe our first interroga-tions. The two-way mirrors don't work. The detainees stare at us as we make our way down the hall. Mortars land outside and we scurry into one of Abu Ghraib's concrete buildings.

We are taken back to the ICE, where we receive our work assign-ments. Bagdasarov and I are put to work immediately. I am assigned to the team responsible for debriefing former regime elements. These are the men who worked closely with Saddam Hussein. Henson works with me as an analyst. It's never entirely clear how the Army determines whether any of us have the proper security clearance. Some employees are told they have "interim clearances." Others are told they'll receive theirs soon. Others aren't told anything. No one from the Army ever asks. No one from the Army ever requests doc-umentation. We let CACI handle it. I am handed a folder and told to be ready to get to work first thing tomorrow morning.

I walk back to the cell where we sleep. I pass by the dining facility, which isn't serving hot food. Loud pops. Some scurry for cover. Some don't. Those who don't seek cover laugh at those who do. They say, "That's outgoing, not incoming." These are U.S. Army 120mm mortar teams. They are positioned in an open field not far from the dining facility. I watch and listen as they send mortars out into the neighborhoods surrounding Abu Ghraib.

I walk past Camp Ganci. Peter Ganci was a NYC firefighter killed on 9/11. The army has named a detention facility inside Abu Ghraib after him. Ganci holds four thousand prisoners. They live in tents. There are concrete bunkers near the edge of the camp where they can hide during mortar attacks. I stand near the barbed-wire fence. Prisoners gather and stare. The crowd grows. A young soldier in a guard tower says, "Careful sir, I only have a few rounds." I walk away. There is a single incoming mortar round. The prisoners don't run to the concrete bunkers.

5.4

It is Sunday. I'm scheduled to conduct my first interrogation. The Army has set up a room full of computers, adjacent to the dining facility, where soldiers can access email and the Internet. The Army calls this an Internet café, but it is nothing more than a bunch of dusty desks and old Dell computers. I stand in line for fifteen minutes of Internet time. It's just enough to download one email from my sister. My four-year-old nephew had to be taken to the emergency room. He stuck a bean up his nose and couldn't blow it out. Thirty miles away, in Baghdad, a suicide bomber detonates a vehicle and kills more than twenty Iraqis.

From the Internet café, I walk to the ICE. There is a large expanse of macadam where Army helicopters land to deliver prisoners. I watch a mushroom cloud rise above the walls of Abu Ghraib as ordnance-disposal teams detonate an IED. I pass by the makeshift chapel. I have time for the opening hymn. I sing "Blessed Be the Tie That Binds." I place the hymnal under the folding chair and reach for my body armor. I work the Velcro straps on the armor as slowly as possible, so as not to disturb the other worshipers. The straps make a terrible tearing sound.

On my way to the ICE, I stop and rest near the HESCO barriers near Camp Ganci. I pray. I've not pursued prayer in some time. But as I sit in a prison in Iraq and prepare to interrogate prisoners of war, it seems appropriate to pray to God. Presbyterians are taught to pray with the Lord's Prayer in mind. We begin with praise, then move on to requests and confessions before closing with words of thanks. My prayer outside Camp Ganci ends quickly. As I move toward requests, I feel a terrible sense of shame. I cannot ask God to accompany me into the interrogation booth.

In Scripture, God often works in prisons, but he is never on the side of the jailer. He is always on the side of the prisoner. The realization brings on a physical reaction. My hands shake. My face warms. I feel nauseated. The sensation is terrifying. Prayer in Iraq is dangerous. I am beginning to realize I'm not on God's path. I'm on my own.

Henson walks by on his way to the ICE. He says "Let's go, Jesus, time for work."

5.5

Henson and I sort through dozens of manila folders containing information on the men I've been assigned to interrogate. We know nothing about any of them. The screeners who conducted the initial intake interviews determined that these men were associated with Saddam's regime, but how, why, or at what level remains unclear. Henson says he'll spend the day reading up on the files and try to work out whom we should be spending the most time with. He closes his eyes, pulls a folder from the middle of the pile, and says, "In the meantime, good luck."

There is no discussion of policy or procedure. As at the processing center at Fort Bliss, and the convoy briefing at Camp Victory, everyone is left to essentially carve out their own way forward. As a contractor, I'm expected to know how to do the job. But I don't.

I wait in a plywood interrogation booth while soldiers locate and deliver my first prisoner. In the booth are three plastic chairs and a plywood table. A steel hook is embedded in the floor. One of the chairs has plastic zip ties secured to the rear legs. My Arabic isn't yet strong enough to let me conduct interrogations on my own, so I work with a translator from Sudan. I struggle to understand his English.

A young soldier working as an MP escorts an old detainee into the room. Like all prisoners, he is handcuffed and hooded. I remove the hood from his head. The MP struggles with the lock on the handcuffs. He drops them and they fall to the floor. The detainee reaches down and picks them up for him. The young MP says, "I'll be right outside."

The ICE has provided every interrogator with a list of critical questions that need answers. These are called priority intelligence requirements (PIRs). PIRs are written by different units and cover a variety of topics. Smaller units may want specific information on the threat level of a particular intersection. Larger units may want information on entire villages or towns, while the top-echelon groups look for trends and demographics.

The most important PIR in January 2004, however, is information on the location of chemical weapons. I prepare a list of questions based on the PIRs. I ask: Sunni or Shia? Baath party? What level? Occupation? Rank? Family? Sons? How many weapons in your house? How many weapons in your car? Why were you detained by Coalition forces? Did you fight during the invasion? What do you know about the regime's chemical weapons program?

The answers are "Sunni," "Yes," "Firqa," "Driver," "Sergeant," "Three children," "Two sons," "One," "One," "I don't understand," "I went home," "I don't understand."

My Sudanese translator struggles to understand my English. The detainee struggles to understand the dialect of the translator. The translator struggles to understand the Arabic of the detainee. I struggle to understand the English of the translator. It takes nearly two hours to collect enough information to write a report that says, "Detainee doesn't seem to understand questions about chemical weapons."

For the next week, I interrogate men who cannot understand my translator. I write short reports that detail the detainees' military records and service in the Baath party. They all have weapons in their households and they all deserted their units and went home during the invasion. None of them know why they have been detained. None of them understand the question about chemical weapons. At the end of each report, there is a section where the interrogator offers an assessment of how great a threat the detainee poses to Coalition forces. For the first week at Abu Ghraib, I misunderstand this question. I assume that it refers to the threat level inside the prison. None of the men I interrogate seems to pose a threat to Army personnel inside the prison. At the bottom of each report I write, "Detainee is not a threat to Coalition forces."

Eventually my supervisor pulls me aside and explains that this is a recommendation for release. There is an interrogator at Abu Ghraib who is assigned to review reports and process detainees for release from the prison. When reports indicate that detainees do not pose a threat to Coalition forces, the reports are sent to him for approval. He meets with me about the large number of detainees I've accidentally recommended for release. I explain my confusion. He says, "I figured it was something like that." He returns all of my files. I do not want to appear as though I do not know what I'm doing. On my next interrogation report I write, "Detainee is a threat to Coalition forces."

The Iraqi dialect is difficult to pick up, but not as difficult as the Sudanese dialect. After two weeks I find myself translating for the translators. Their Arabic is enough to point the detainee in the right direction; my Arabic is enough to finish the questioning. I begin to learn a great deal about Iraq, the Baath party, Saddam Hussein, Abu Ghraib, the Iran-Iraq War, Sunnis and Shiites, and the Iraqi military. In those first few weeks, I don't answer one PIR.

At night, the five of us return to our cell and pretend we aren't at Abu Ghraib. We make fun of Blee for being too young. We make fun of Bagdasarov for being a Communist. They make fun of me for writing in my journal and being a pastor. I tell them I was rejected by seminary. They make fun of me for this, too. We make fun of Henson for not knowing the difference between Iran and Iraq. No one makes fun of Kutcher.

We disappear into headphones and drown ourselves in music. Kutcher steals our headphones and tells the others what we are listening to. We laugh at Blee for Britney Spears and the Black Eyed Peas. We laugh at Bagdasarov for Harry Chapin. I take significant punishment for Amy Grant and Michael W. Smith. I'm given some credit for Zeppelin, but then Kutcher finds Sinéad O'Connor. He says, "I thought you loved Jesus. Faggots can't love Jesus." Kutcher and Henson are happy to show us their music. They introduce us to System of a Down. It is aggressive and deafening. I enjoy being surrounded by friends.

5.6

I make other friends, too. Friends like Ferdinand Ibabao.

Ferdinand is a former police officer from Guam. He served in the U.S. Army's 25th Infantry Division. I meet him for the first time in mid-January, during a convoy back to Baghdad to collect supplies from CACIville. Kutcher recruited him to be our driver. Ferdinand is overweight. He makes fun of himself for this. But Ferdinand is not soft. He is strong and intimidating. He has thick black hair and a dark complexion. We make fun of him for looking like a fat Iraqi insurgent, but only because he allows it.

Ferdinand tells funny stories. He has his own catchphrase. When he slows down and says, "Hey, man," you know he is about to tell you the best part of the story.

He tells this story about driving back through the gates of Abu Ghraib after a supply run to Camp Victory. He says U.S. soldiers in the guard tower mistook him for an Iraqi driver. He says "Hey, man." They ordered him to stop, but he thought they were shouting at another vehicle, so he drove faster. They fired warning shots into his engine block. Now, when Ferdinand's coming back into Abu Ghraib, we make him hide in the backseat under a blanket.

In late January, Ferdinand and I ride together during a convoy back to Baghdad. I'm glad to have him in the vehicle. I drive while he handles the foreign-made weapons. We head out onto the roads of Iraq and avoid the U.S. Army convoys, which have become frequent targets of IEDs. We buy liquor in Baghdad and deliver it to the soldiers stationed at Abu Ghraib. In return, the soldiers give us access to large caches of captured weaponry. The entire transaction is illegal in the eyes of the military, but no one cares, and no one disapproves. It's a fair exchange for everyone involved. Ferdinand knows a great deal about foreign weapons. He chooses the best. We head back out onto the roads of Iraq with other CACI employees and stop on an isolated stretch of highway so we can test-fire the weapons into a highway berm.

On one return trip to Abu Ghraib, we encounter an Army convoy that has been struck by an IED. The explosive device was buried in the road and paved over. There are no injuries but the lead vehicle has been disabled. The convoy is waiting for reinforcements before advancing on a series of buildings in the distance whose occupants must have known something about the IED and the highway equipment used to conceal it. They say there are almost certainly more IEDs down the road.

Ferdinand insists that we move forward. The driver of another vehicle says we should either stay put or head back to Baghdad and wait until the road is cleared. Ferdinand says the road is never cleared. Ferdinand says the worst thing we can do is stay with the Army convoy because it will attract small-arms fire. We have no armor. Eventually the other driver decides to return to Baghdad.

That night at the prison, CACI leadership calls a meeting to discuss the incident on the road. A shouting match ensues about one group leaving another group behind. Someone says we need to follow orders. Someone else says no orders were given. There is another argument about whether or not we take orders from the Army. Ferdinand says, "You're not soldiers anymore. You don't give orders, you don't take orders." Someone says, "Who gives orders in the interrogation booth?" No one has an answer for this.

5.7

Throughout the first two weeks of January, I go back to the interrogation booth and fail to answer PIRs. I turn in reports that say, "Detainee is a threat to Coalition forces." Most interrogators are having the same results and writing the same reports. We begin to question the process.

There are doubts about the number and quality of the detainees being processed at Abu Ghraib. There are doubts about the effectiveness of an interrogation program that prohibits interrogators from spending more than an hour or two with any one detainee. There are doubts about the presence of chemical weapons. There are doubts about the security of the prison. The number of detainees at Abu Ghraib is growing. The number of interrogators is not. There are thousands of detainees who will never be processed. But there are no doubts or questions about the way we are handling detainees. My interrogations have been direct and civil. Like any interrogator, I'm certain prisoners have lied to me, but I don't have any means or reason to retaliate for this. There are too many interrogations to conduct. I simply move on to the next prisoner. I've raised my voice and become argumentative in the booth, but in January 2004, I have no reason to believe I or anyone else has done anything wrong.

Soon that will change. Higher-ups are not satisfied with results coming out of Abu Ghraib. We are still struggling to find chemical weapons. The number of IEDs and mortar attacks is increasing at an alarming rate throughout the country. Coalition forces are beginning to take casualties the way they did during the invasion. There is talk that fighting may last through the summer.

The Army calls a meeting in the ICE. The captain and the first sergeant stand up front and lead a class on interrogation techniques. They talk about planning and preparation, the approach phase, the questioning phase, and the termination phase. There is a lecture about proper reporting and paperwork. They hand out copies of the Army field manual covering interrogations. Every Army job has a "how-to" field manual. There are field manuals on cleaning weapons, maintaining military vehicles, and properly wearing the uniforms. There are always soldiers who can tell you exactly what the field manuals say. They tell you what it says about your uniform violation, or that you're using an unauthorized tool to clean your weapon, or that you failed to give your vehicle's engine enough time to warm up. The soldiers who rely on field manuals are called barracks lawyers. No one likes barracks lawyers. No one likes field manuals.

When the captain and first sergeant finish with the refresher class, another soldier stands up front and reads a directive about the proper way to spell "Abu Ghraib" on our interrogation reports. There must be uniformity. There are questions about this. Some say it needs to be spelled with a "y." Others insist there should be a silent "e." There is talk of teaching everyone how to write it out in Arabic script. Someone wants to know what the field manual says. This discussion goes on for nearly an hour. We'll revisit the proper spelling of Abu Ghraib in future meetings.

We take a break and reconvene for another class on creative solutions. The first sergeant says you can't just read questions. You can't just be a robot. You need to be creative. He talks about Hanns Scharff. Scharff was a German interrogator during World War II who questioned downed American pilots. He was fluent in English. He took his prisoners for walks through the woods. He befriended them. He gained confidence. He acquired information. After the war, his former prisoners invited him to Christmas dinner in the United States. He became an American citizen and eventually taught interrogation techniques to the U.S. military. The first sergeant tells us to emulate Hanns Scharff. He says, "It doesn't mean take your prisoners for a walk in the woods. It means to think outside the fucking manual." The first sergeant introduces a civilian interrogator who has been getting results. He says we should pay attention and learn from the guys who are managing to get things done. He introduces Steven Stefanowicz.

5.8

I see what's outside the fucking manual for the first time later in the day, during my first visit to the hard site. Steven Stefanowicz takes me on a tour of the hard site. He chooses me because I speak Arabic, have a security clearance, and worked for the NSA. He says, "You're the kind of person we need working on the guys in the hard site." The hard site contains a relatively small number of Iraqi prisoners who have been deemed more valuable than the thousands of others languishing in the outdoor camps. The interrogators who work with detainees inside the hard site often spend weeks, as opposed to hours, questioning their targets. Those of us who haven't been inside the hard site think of it as a better work environment than the cold plywood interrogation booths.

The hard site is a two-tiered building with an open bay running down the middle allowing full view of all the cells. As Stefanowicz leads me into the building, I see naked men. There are naked men in the cells. Naked men handcuffed to chairs outside the cells. Naked men standing in lines. There is a man on the floor who is being told to get naked. When he refuses, someone grabs him by his pants and drags him along the floor on his back. The pants come off and he is naked. The hard site is cold. Stefanowicz waits while I return to the ICE to retrieve my jacket.

Stefanowicz takes me to a windowless cell where he and an analyst have been working on a detainee. This detainee is from Yemen. The cell is long and narrow. I hear muffled music from inside the cell. There are two doors, one behind the other. Both doors are covered in plywood and spray-painted black. You can close the first door before opening the second. That way, you ensure no light enters the cell. Today, Stefanowicz opens both doors. The music is louder. Stefanowicz shuts it off and has a short conversation with a naked detainee. He tells him he will see him tomorrow. In Arabic, the detainee says, "Please, please, spend more time, no music, a little more time." The translator turns the music back on. Stefanowicz says, "Annoying stuff, right?" He closes both doors and says, "We'll let him stew for a few days."

I tell Stefanowicz about System of a Down. I say, "Deafening crap, just total crap." Stefanowicz tells me that is exactly what he's looking for. I tell him I'll talk to Kutcher and Henson.

We walk back through the hard site and I see more things.

Stefanowicz says once I spend a few weeks learning the basics with the former regime element (FRE) guys I'll be able to come in here and help him out. He says, "We need your language. We need to be able to talk to these guys on our own." Then Stefanowicz shows me how to fill out the paperwork to gain approval for this type of interrogation. He says never to proceed without approval. We fill out forms and use words like "exposure," "sound," "light," "cold," "food," and "isolation." We put them in a bin where they'll wait for signatures. Stefanowicz says, "Be creative. Don't be stupid."

Later that afternoon, I have lunch with Ferdinand. We've agreed to meet and talk about the IED incident on the highway and the CACI meeting that ensued. We agree we made the right decision about moving forward on the road. We end up talking about Steven Stefanowicz. Ferdinand doesn't think Stefanowicz is qualified to do the job. He thinks he may have faked his résumé. He says, "You know the type." He tells me not to spend time with Stefanowicz. He says, "Hey, man, keep your distance." He tells me to stay away from the hard site.

I never go back inside the hard site. I try not to remember the things I didn't like. The smell is something I try not to remember. The sound is something I try not to remember. The naked man is something I try not to remember. The dark cell is something I try not to remember. I gave Stefanowicz a copy of the deafening music. I try not to remember that, either.

5.9

The rains of January turn Abu Ghraib to mud. They quiet the mortar attacks, but only briefly. Interrogations continue. I speak to old men who have been detained because of their connections to the young men who are doing the fighting. I speak to young men who have been detained because of their connections to the old men who tell the young men whom to fight. I speak to Iraqi Army officers who trained young Iraqi soldiers how to fire rocket-propelled grenades (RPGs). When I ask the Iraqi officers whether they've ever fired an RPG at an American vehicle, they say, "No, I don't know about RPGs." I speak with Iraqi businessmen who import washing-machine timers from Iran to be used as detonators for IEDs. They say they don't know anything about IEDs. Then they say IEDs are set off with cell phones. I speak with Iraqis who have been captured with large numbers of cell phones. They tell me IEDs are set off with simple timers used in everyday appliances like washing machines. I speak with Iraqis who have been detained for housing large numbers of young men from Jordan and Saudi Arabia. The Iraqis say these men are on pilgrimage. It is their duty to house them. In Baghdad, young men from Jordan and Saudi Arabia drive explosives-laden vehicles into American and Iraqi checkpoints. I speak to Iraqis who have been captured with mortar tubes. The Iraqis say they stole the tubes from a military armory or found them abandoned on the side of the road or took them along when they defected or found them buried in a farm field. They were going to sell the mortar tubes for scrap. The rain stops falling. The mortars fall instead.

One evening I walk from the ICE to the dining facility with Blee and Bagdasarov. Halfway between the ICE and the dining facility, in a muddy and exposed portion of the prison, we hear the sound of incoming rounds. The incoming rounds land close. I feel heat and mud on my face. The detonation fills my clothes with a puff of air like a sudden breeze in a storm. There is a pause, then more rounds. Blee, Bagdasarov, and I have a conversation. The ground around us is damp and muddy. There is no laundry service at Abu Ghraib. We do not want to get our clothes dirty, so we decide to keep walking.

We make it to a concrete shelter and crowd in with some soldiers. Outside we see other soldiers talking about the mortars. They are still walking toward the shelter. Most mortar attacks are brief, but this one drags on. The detonations intensify. It becomes a full-scale artillery attack. Each flash of light illuminates the growing cloud of smoke produced by previous rounds. Tracer rounds engulf a nearby guard tower. Rounds sail overhead, producing a high-pitched *wisp*. A Katyusha rocket streaks and growls overhead. An IED targets American vehicles as they race to respond outside the prison. I feel the detonation in my teeth. Those still outside the bunker are either lying in the mud or running toward the shelter.

The next morning, I conduct an interrogation. The detainee is said to be a member of Ansar al-Islam, one of the many umbrella groups that incorporate former Iraqi army soldiers who want to fight Coalition forces. They are known to launch mortars into Abu Ghraib. The detainee does not hide his affiliation or his actions. He was caught with mortar rounds. He says the reason we can't catch them is they drive their mortar teams around on the back of flatbed trucks. As soon as they launch their rounds, they drive to a new location before launching more. He laughs about the incoming rounds from the previous night. He insists there will be more.

This is the first detainee I lay hands on. I grab him by his clothing and drag him out of his chair. He is lighter than I expected, and I shove him into the wall far more violently than I intended. But I am thinking of the mortar attacks, and I am thinking about how scared I am, and I am thinking he deserves this. He does, and it feels good. This is the first interrogation for which I fill out the paperwork Stefanowicz showed me. This is the first interrogation where I answer a PIR.

Later that week, three detainees are killed in another artillery strike on Abu Ghraib. Many more are wounded, as are two U.S. soldiers. In late January, I get my first day off in more than a month. I stand in line at a newly installed phone facility and call Karin for the first time since a brief phone call from Camp Victory. There is a significant delay and the conversation is difficult to follow. I focus on her voice. The sound is soothing and soft. It makes me feel guilty; I hang up. Later, I send an email and say the connection must have broken. I stay in touch with Karin through emails, but I never again call her from Abu Ghraib.

More mortars strike the prison. I lay my hands on more detainees. I fill out more paperwork. I answer more PIRs. I try to forget Karin's voice.

Henson and I work well together. He earns a reputation as a dependable intelligence analyst. He is given the opportunity to work in the hard site alongside Steven Stefanowicz. I tell him to be careful. I tell him what Ferdinand said. I continue my work in the plywood interrogation booths.

The MPs deliver a detainee who was captured with Iraqi propaganda videos. The videos show old footage of Iraqi army units marching in parades and navigating obstacle courses. An Iraqi man dressed in traditional Arab garments sings the praises of Saddam Hussein and the homeland of Iraq. The video encourages Iraqis to rise up and defend their country. We stand around and laugh at it.

The MPs shove the detainee as he enters the room. The detainee stumbles and falls. One of the MPs throws a plastic lawn chair at him. They wrestle the hood from his head, stand him up, and shove him into the chair. He topples over and falls back to the floor. I sit in the corner and fill out paperwork, pretending not to care.

The plywood interrogation booths offer no protection from the January winds. They also offer no protection from the sounds that come from adjacent booths. As my detainee shivers in the plastic lawn chair, we both sit and listen to the things going on next door. There is shouting and the sound of something crashing into a wall. Maybe a person. A man sobs.

I learn to leave the room during the worst of the sounds. I place a hood over my detainees, secure their feet to the iron loop in the floor, and abandon them to their own imaginations. I sit outside in the quiet. I return and remove the hood.

5.10

I'm assigned a group of four men who were captured at a checkpoint by U.S. forces. They were driving a vehicle with a corpse in the trunk. There is a photograph of the corpse. There is no information about any of the men.

I interrogate each of the men individually. The driver tells me the corpse in the trunk is his uncle. He was murdered during a business trip to Ramadi. They were taking him back to Baghdad for burial. In separate interrogations, the remaining three men offer the same story. They know the corpse's name, they know the corpse's family members, they know where the corpse worked, they know when the corpse served in the Iraqi army, they know the corpse was arrested by secret police in 1998, they know the corpse celebrated Saddam's capture, and they had dinner with the corpse before he left for the trip to Ramadi. They ate the cookies called kleicha. The corpse's wife makes a special kind of kleicha. They all want to know what happened to the corpse. Was their uncle buried properly?

I interrogate a businessman from Karbala. His neighbors suspected him of anti-Coalition activity and turned him in. He admits to being a member of the Baath party. He says everyone is a member of the Baath party. He says you can't do business unless you agree to become a member of the Baath party. He says his neighbors are members of the Baath party, too. Their business interests conflicted with his. They got him arrested so they could take over his business. He shows me the scars on his ears. He deserted the army during the war against Iran, was arrested by Saddam's intelligence services, and spent three years at Abu Ghraib. He says the prison is different now. He says it's much easier.

I interrogate an Iraqi general. He ordered his unit to surrender to U.S. forces during the invasion. He returned to Baghdad to be with his family. U.S. forces came to his house, looking for one of his sons, and detained him instead. The capture report says, "Detainee is to be released when detainee's son is located." It was written three months ago. The general says, "You've probably killed him by now."

I interrogate an old man. The report mentions "anti-Coalition activities." He says he needs medicine for his kidneys. It takes the translator nearly an hour to determine the name of the medicine. The old man is in pain. He holds his side and moans.

I interrogate an even older man. The translator cannot understand his Arabic. The translator says, "Let's just send this guy home."

I interrogate men who cry when asked about their families. I interrogate men who cry when asked about their parents. I interrogate men who cry when asked about their wives. I interrogate men who cry and ask about when they'll be going home.

I do not lay hands on any of these detainees, as I did to the men who taunted me about the mortar attacks. My questioning is direct and conversational. Some of the men provide information, others do not, but no matter how gentle the interrogation might be, I leave the booth feeling guilty and condemned. None of these men are being protected. They are detained in one of Saddam Hussein's most infamous prisons, they are given no information about their status, and they have no way of knowing when or if they will see their families again. Some of them are guilty; some of them are not. All of them are jailed under intolerable circumstances. I am their jailer. If God is on anyone's side in Iraq, it's not mine.

Bagdasarov and I talk about the sad stories from the interrogation booth. He says he still isn't answering any PIRs. He's not sure his detainees have any real information to offer. He says, "It's not like I'm going to recommend anyone for release or anything, but I'm starting to wonder." He asks me to help him with an interrogation. The detainee is a young man. This is what we call children at Abu Ghraib. Iraqis don't track their birthdays so the vast majority of Iraqis don't know their exact age. They say they are thirty, or forty, or fifty. When they are young, they don't say their age; they say who their father is. We call them young men. They are boys.

The boy is suspected of anti-Coalition activities. He was captured with car batteries and an extensive collection of electronic devices. Car batteries are used to detonate IEDs. Bagdasarov asked the boy about the car batteries. The boy said his father uses the car batteries for fishing. Bagdasarov says, "I don't know enough about Iraq to know if that's true." Neither of us can picture anyone fishing with car batteries. Like many interrogators, Bagdasarov is also having trouble with his translator. He says, "This was so much easier in Bosnia." I agree to help.

I talk to the boy about car batteries and I ask about fishing. I ask about what types of fish he is catching. I ask him what he does with the fish, how he stores them, how he transports them, and where he sells them. I ask him the best way to clean a fish. I ask him about gutting a fish. The boy knows nothing about fishing. I lay hands on the boy. I scare him. I shout. I throw a chair. It ricochets off the wall. I call the MP inside and he handcuffs the boy to the iron loop in the floor. We leave him there. We return. I remove the handcuffs and give him instructions on how to sit in the electric chair position that devastated us in boot camp. He lasts only a few minutes before slumping onto the ground. I make him stand up, lift his arms in the air, place heavy folders in his hands, and tell him to keep them above his head. I tell him to wait. He suffers. He cries. I make him lie down on the floor. I roll him to the left and the right. I tell him to roll on his own. He is filthy. He is crying. His father, he says, doesn't use the batteries for fishing. He delivers them to men but he doesn't know what for. I say, "Car bombs." He says, "Yes, yes." I bring in a map of his neighborhood. The boy shows me where the shop is.

Later, Bagdasarov and I hear that when the shop was raided, half a dozen vehicles were discovered in different stages of preparation to become car bombs. Large amounts of explosives along with various types of detonators (including car batteries) were discovered as well. Three young men with Jordanian passports were found living in a shack in an adjacent field.

Other detainees tell this same story about using car batteries for fishing, and I do the same thing to all the men who tell me this story. They cry and ask to go home. I don't get any more results. I tell Randy Kutcher the ridiculous story about men who claim to fish with car batteries and the kid whose dad ran the car-bomb shop. I tell him how I'm not falling for that bullshit anymore and how I go after the guys who tell it. He says, "You asshole, of course they fish with car batteries. I used to do it in Georgia." At Abu Ghraib I stop laying my hands on detainees, I stop using stress positions, and I stop shoving prisoners into walls.

Henson overhears the conversation with Kutcher. He's been

working in the hard site the last few days, doing research on a detainee from Yemen who has been recruiting young men to fight in Iraq. He says he's not so sure about what Stefanowicz is doing. He's tired of hearing the detainees cry and beg for food, or light, or silence. He says, "I'd rather just come back and work with you guys."

I've seen enough of Abu Ghraib. I begin to question CACI leadership about my stay here. I want to know when I'll be sent back to Baghdad. But CACI managers at Abu Ghraib say I'm doing well in the booth. They've heard good things. They heard about the Ansar al-Islam guy and the car batteries and the guys with the Jordanian passports. I'm making a difference. They'd be happy to let me work out my contract at Abu Ghraib.

5.11

In late January, everyone working at Abu Ghraib is ordered to schedule a meeting with an agent from the Army's Criminal Investigation Command (CID). The investigators are part of a team that has been sent to Abu Ghraib to investigate claims of detainee abuse. We've heard there are pictures. Bagdasarov, Henson, and I are assigned similar time slots to visit CID. We walk across the prison complex together and speculate about what they're looking for. Bagdasarov asks about the hard site. Henson says, "Don't ask."

The CID office includes a waiting room with chairs. When we walk in, two soldiers from the FRE team are waiting their turns. A CID agent no older than John Blee calls my name, leads me to a small room, and closes the door. I ask him whether I am free to leave. He says, "Not yet." I tell him this means I am under arrest. I tell him to read me my rights. He says it doesn't work that way in the Army. I tell him I'm not in the Army. I ask him to open the door. He refuses, so I stand up and open it myself. We argue about whether or not I am subject to military law. He is frustrated. He tells me to relax. He says, "If you know something, now's the time." He asks about Steven Stefanowicz. He asks about dogs. He hands me a paper and tells me to check the appropriate boxes.

I head back out to the waiting room, where I find Bagdasarov. Henson and the two soldiers from the FRE team are still being interviewed. Eventually, Henson and one of the soldiers join us in the waiting room. We all agree to wait for the other soldier. The young CID agent tells us to move along. We tell him we want to wait for our friend. He says, "What friend? No one else is here."

The other soldier is cooperating with investigators. Only later will CID recognize they cannot allow potential sources to sit in a waiting room together. The waiting room is eventually eliminated, but not before everyone at the prison is able to figure out who spent extra time talking to CID. A few months later, in April, the U.S. secretary of defense, Donald Rumsfeld, will publicly thank Sergeant Joe Darby for providing photographs of abuse at Abu Ghraib to Criminal Investigation Command. Prior to this, no one knew who provided the photographs. The Army will then place Darby in protective custody.

"What are you going to tell Karin about this?" This is what Ferdinand asks me in the dining facility. We were talking about our interviews with the agents. Neither of us checked the appropriate boxes on that piece of paper to indicate something was wrong at Abu Ghraib. Ferdinand had the young agent, too. He went through the same door-closing routine, but eventually he just got up and left. Now he's wondering if he shouldn't go back and check some of the boxes. He wonders what he'll tell his wife and son.

Three years from now, I'll see that piece of paper with the appropriate boxes again. A Department of Justice prosecutor and two CID agents will question me about an article I publish in the *Washington Post*. The article will address some of the things I did at Abu Ghraib, but it won't reveal everything. One of the agents will pull out this piece of paper and say, "Remember this?" He'll ask me why I didn't check the appropriate boxes. I will say, "I'm not proud of that."

5.12

In late January, I transition onto a new interrogation team. The Army is working to reorganize the structure in order to address growing concerns about the men planting IEDs in the roads. Convoys are beginning to take heavy casualties. Henson and Blee have been assigned to small teams of CACI personnel who will join front-line troops in order to provide more direct interrogation services for units stationed outside of Abu Ghraib.

In February, the five of us drive back to Baghdad one last time to purchase liquor for Henson and Blee before they leave Abu Ghraib. We eat at the new Burger King trailer that has been flown in and set up at Camp Victory. We eat at the Bob Hope Dining Facility, where there is a hamburger bar. They grill you a hamburger and let you add your own choice of toppings. They have hot peppers and bacon, cold soda and ice cream. We visit CACIville and take hot showers. We shit in the clean portable toilets. We visit the PX and buy Gatorade and Doritos. We drive back to Abu Ghraib, where we stand on the roof of a prison building and toast the departure of Blee and Henson. Blee is scared. He says, "Maybe it's time to just go home." We say, "It can't be worse than Abu Ghraib." Mortar rounds chase us back inside.

That night someone shines a light in my eyes. A man is standing over me and asking me questions. He asks me my name. I shove his flashlight out of the way. He apologizes. He says he's heard of me. I speak Arabic. I produce in the booth. I keep to myself. He introduces himself as Brent Jennings, the lead interrogator for the team headed to Fallujah. He says the other interrogator they had assigned isn't willing to make the trip. He's a pussy, not cut out for this sort of thing. There needs to be an immediate answer. We leave tomorrow. Yes or no, in or out?

6

In the morning, I regret the decision to leave for Fallujah. I think about what Blee said about going home. I plot out my departure and estimate the number of days it will take to leave Iraq and be back in bed with Karin. It will take six days; one full day to get back to Baghdad, one day in Baghdad to schedule a flight to Kuwait, one day in Kuwait to reserve a flight back to Texas, two days in Texas to turn in gear, and one day of travel back to Bethlehem. Six days. I tell myself that I should make an effort to last another six days. At the end of six days, I can reevaluate and make the decision to go home. I will survive the rest of Iraq by surviving the next six days, then the next six days, then the next.

Ferdinand is going to Fallujah with us. Like me, he received a late-night visit from Brent after another screener dropped out. The departure to Fallujah is delayed when Brent is told to arrive ahead of the team in order to secure living arrangements. One of the analysts on the team, Jim Fisk, convinces Brent that he should take another person to act as his second in command. Jim volunteers himself for the position.

Jim is young. He is tall with broad shoulders. Like Ferdinand, he is overweight. Unlike Ferdinand, he carries the weight awkwardly.

But he is also well spoken, masking the incompetence that will eventually come to define him and our interaction in Fallujah and beyond. This is the first time Jim inserts himself into a position he isn't qualified to fill. It won't be the last.

While Brent and Jim move west, the four of us who remain behind tell each other that Fallujah cannot be worse than Abu Ghraib. We occupy an empty cell and wait for follow-on orders from Brent and Jim. We expect to leave the next morning, but two full days go by. The days are empty and dull. Our departure is imminent, so CACI doesn't assign us any work. It is the longest stretch of inactivity I've experienced in over a month. On the second night, I have my first nightmare.

In this nightmare, which recurs often, someone I know begins to shrink. At first I can hold them in my hand or put them on a table, but as they grow smaller I begin to lose track of them. They slip through my fingers and disappear onto the floor. I know they're still there but I cannot find them. I hear their screams in my panic as I scramble to avoid stepping on them.

Eventually, Brent and Jim finish the preparation in Fallujah and send for the rest of the team. CACI decides that it is best we do not drive our own vehicles into Fallujah. CACI is concerned about damaging the vehicles they leased in Kuwait. CACI buys used cars to replace the more expensive Toyota Land Cruisers. CACI doesn't issue radios or communication equipment. CACI tells us to travel with the Army.

When we talk about CACI, we never really know whom we are talking about. None of us had a face-to-face job interview or visited the corporate offices in Virginia. None of us met the employees who recruited us. None of us even know what "CACI" stands for. In Iraq, there are CACI employees who hold job titles such as "country manager" or "site supervisor," but they never have answers to our questions. At meetings, they say things like "You'll know as soon as I know" or "We're working on it" or "Just let things work themselves out." After the meetings, we share rumors about the changes CACI is making. We hear about vehicles, or weapons, or body armor, or bonuses. We go back to the site supervisor or country manager and tell him about the rumors. Then there is another meeting, at which the site supervisor or country manager addresses the rumors. Sometimes the rumors turn out to be true, sometimes they don't. Then the country manager or site supervisor tells everyone to calm down. He'll tell us he's trying to get in touch with corporate offices about the other rumors.

The insurgency has been growing steadily since our arrival in Iraq in early January. We hear about the attacks at morning briefs, and the stories get more and more violent. The groups conducting the attacks grow larger, and the attacks grow more frequent. By February 2004, there is little doubt about the lethality of the organized resistance sweeping across Iraq. Abu Ghraib is a dangerous place, to be sure, but the road out west to Fallujah is an all-out meat grinder. Armored vehicles are still uncommon in Iraq, and though soldiers have welded metal plating to the cab of our truck, the back is protected only by the canvas covering designed to keep out the rain.

The Army calls its passengers "packs." There are four of us. An Army sergeant assigns us to the back of a truck. He tells the driver there will be four packs in the cargo area. There are no seats. We ride in the back and sit on cardboard boxes filled with bottled water. When the CACI site supervisor at Abu Ghraib arrives to see us off, we remind him about the armored vehicles and weapons all of us were promised by CACI recruiters. The site supervisor says, "We're working on it."

The Army sergeant says we have to leave our foreign weapons behind. In 2004, thirty-eight civilian contractors are abducted in Iraq. Fourteen of them are subsequently killed. Four others are never heard from again. But the vast majority of contractors are forbidden from carrying government-issued weapons. When we travel on our own, the Army looks the other way and we can keep our illegal weapons, but when we convoy with the military, the Army enforces the rules. CACI has failed to secure the authorization necessary to allow its employees to legally carry weapons in Iraq. We ask the site manager at Abu Ghraib about the weapons policy. We tell him we're pretty sure we're being targeted, even though we are considered noncombatants and Iraqi insurgents are officially not permitted to target us. He tells us CACI is still working on the weapons policy.

As we drive out of Abu Ghraib, the hard site and the interrogation booths are the last things we see. They disappear behind the prison walls as we wind our way through concrete barriers out onto the main road. Abu Ghraib shrinks on the horizon as we travel west to Fallujah.

6.1

In early February 2004, Jim greets us at Camp St. Mere Eglise in Fallujah. The camp is occupied by the Army's 82nd Airborne Division and named after a French town liberated by the 82nd in World War II. Later, in March, the Marines will take over from the Army and rename it Camp Fallujah. In April, the Marines will lay siege to Fallujah in response to the killings of Blackwater employees. In November, during Operation Phantom Fury, they'll all but reduce Fallujah to rubble.

Jim leads us into the building where we will conduct interrogations. It is small. The facility itself is designed to hold approximately one hundred prisoners. There are two offices, one for the military police and one for military intelligence. Two rooms are set aside for interrogation, another for screening, and a third for what Jim calls "other activities." Brent meets me inside the office and pulls me aside. He says, "You're going to love it here, nothing like Abu Ghraib, you can do pretty much anything."

The office is decorated with maps of Fallujah and other nearby cities—Ramadi, Haditha. There are plush black leather chairs and four Dell desktop computers, which rest on makeshift plywood desks. Captain Dent, the officer in charge of the interrogation element at the base, is sitting at one of the computers. She's playing Minesweeper.

Dent clicks on the wrong square and detonates a mine. She says, "No fucking way, bullshit. Fuck." She turns in her chair and sort of waves us in with her fingers. She doesn't stand up. Dent is small and skinny. Ferdinand calls her an ugly cunt under his breath. I laugh.

Dent starts in on the officer's speech. Ferdinand and I have heard it before, as enlisted soldiers. Officers give this speech when they take command of new troops. The officer tells the enlisted personnel not to think of them as an officer. The officer says the enlisted personnel just need to do their jobs. The officer says they won't get in the way. The officer is not a micromanager. Then the officer says something like "There's another side to this coin." This is what Dent says. She says, "There's another side to the coin." That's the officer's warning: Don't force me to step in. Dent says, "Don't make me be the dick."

At Abu Ghraib, it was never clear who was in charge. There were officers, but none of them acted like one. When Dent gives her officer speech, it is clear she is in charge. It is the first time I've encountered someone willing to take responsibility for a group of interrogators in Iraq. We do the work. She takes the professional credit. If we screw up, she takes the professional blame. This is actually the way the Army is supposed to work. I don't like Dent. But Dent acts like an officer, and I respect her for it.

However, the relationship between contractors and soldiers remains unclear. Not only does Captain Dent treat us like soldiers, she treats us like enlisted soldiers. As an officer, she outranks all enlisted personnel, no matter their rank, including those with far more time in service. There are criminal consequences for enlisted soldiers who do not follow her orders. But it's not clear what consequences civilians would face for disobeying Dent.

Dent is telling stories about mortar attacks. She says, "Fucking hajjis can't shoot worth shit." Ferdinand is looking at the maps on the wall. Dent says, "That's fucking Haditha. Fucking Haditha. You'll learn all about that shit hole." Ferdinand picks up a small plywood chair. He says, "What's this?"

The small plywood chair sits on top of a canvas Army cot. It is two feet tall, six inches wide. The legs of the chair are made of two-by-fours. There are plastic zip ties connected to each one. Someone has used a black marker to write an Arabic word on the chair. Jim says the word means "chair." It doesn't. It means "wait."

Captain Dent tells Ferdinand to ask Staff Sergeant Tyner about the chair. Tyner is one of two U.S. Army interrogators from the 82nd Airborne stationed at the facility. The other is Sergeant Hoagie. Tyner and Hoagie laugh when asked about the chair. They call it the Palestinian chair. They say the Israelis taught them how to build it during a joint training exercise. I assume it's called the Palestinian chair because that's who was forced to sit in it. Tyner and Hoagie tell Ferdinand to try and sit in it. Ferdinand crouches down and squeezes his large frame onto the tiny chair. It forces him to lean forward and support his weight with his legs. We laugh. He says, "Hey, man, what the hell?"

Tyner and Hoagie help Ferdinand stand up and then take a few minutes to show us how to use the chair. Captain Dent looks on as they explain to us how the Palestinian chair works. It takes only a few minutes. The chair forces you to support all of your weight with your thighs. Once they give out, you basically start to suffocate. They say everyone breaks in the chair.

Tyner has an interrogation scheduled. He leaves the office and says he'll meet us at dinner. Brent pulls me aside and says, "Stick around, watch this." We don't see the interrogation. We hear it. Tyner is screaming. There is no translator with him. Tyner doesn't speak Arabic. He just berates the detainee with volume and profanity. Then we hear what I come to understand is the crashing of plastic chairs against the walls, followed by the noise of the plywood desk being torn apart. Brent says, "They've already rebuilt it three times in two days." Then there is the sound of skin slapping skin. Then there is crying. There is Arabic, but I can't understand it. The voice sounds sad and scared. After less than ten minutes, Tyner returns. He says, "That'll get him warmed up."

At dinner, we sit with our military counterparts and talk about how we are meant to work together. Hoagie and Tyner will spend much of their time traveling off base to provide interrogation services to front-line units. Brent and I will be expected to do the same, but only when Hoagie and Tyner aren't available. In the meantime, we can expect to do the bulk of our work on base. There are enough detainees to keep us busy. Jim has volunteered to do interrogations as well. He is an analyst, but he insists he received interrogation training during his four years in the Army. I ask Jim about DLI and he can't tell me what it is. I tell him most Army interrogators are required to graduate from DLI. I tell him the ones who flunk out become analysts. Jim says, "They made an exception for me."

I suspect Jim isn't telling the truth about his interrogation training. I've never heard of an analyst being cross-trained as an interrogator. But Jim has already managed to take his four years in the Army and turn them into a supervisory role with CACI. None of us think of him as a supervisor. None of us listen to him. But the Army officers we work with accept his title. Now he's acting as an interrogator. None of us think of him as one, but the Army accepts this, too. The more positions he assumes, the higher he can climb, and all of it seems to go unchallenged. Jim is an entry-level employee, he barely appears qualified to be an analyst. In Fallujah he serves as second in command. As the war in Iraq drags on, he'll rise even higher.

The camp at Fallujah has an extensive Internet café, far better than the dusty computer room at Abu Ghraib. I check email and find a note from Karin indicating that CACI has failed to deposit my latest paycheck. There have been problems with CACI's payroll services since I left for Fort Bliss in December. Some paychecks have been for too little, others arrived late, and some not at all. Most CACI employees are having similar problems. I haven't spoken to Karin on the phone since I hung up on her at Abu Ghraib. I call her and jump straight into questions about the paycheck. I tell her it's too difficult for me to contact the CACI offices in Virginia. I tell her she needs to call them.

Karin says she is happy to keep the records, and she'll let me know when the paycheck comes in, but she'd rather not take sides in an argument with CACI. I don't have the courage to admit that coming to Iraq has been a mistake, that my actions here are mine alone, so I blame Karin for failing to support me in an argument with CACI. I should be listening to Karin. I should be asking her about life in Bethlehem. I should be valuing her concerns. Instead, I accuse of her of failing to support my needs.

In what remains of that phone call, Karin tries to steer the conversation away from CACI. She asks about Ferdinand and how things are going and what she can send. She tells me it's okay to come home and to not worry about the money. We'll be fine just the way we are. When she says it's nice to hear my voice, I hang up. This is the second time I speak to Karin on the phone from Iraq. It is also the last.

After hanging up on Karin, I return an hour later to check email. I sit at the computer screen and hit the send/receive button. I write an apology and then delete it. I hit send/receive again but nothing appears. Ferdinand comes by and asks if I'm ready to go. I hit send/receive one last time. I convince myself to last another six days.

The next morning I conduct my first interrogation in Fallujah. The young detainee is one of five brothers who were picked up during the same operation. Unlike the prisoners at Abu Ghraib, who were often held for weeks or months before we spoke to them, these men have been in U.S. custody for only a few days. The translator is a naturalized U.S. citizen who grew up in Egypt. His English is solid, but his Egyptian dialect is thick and unpolished. I struggle to understand the Arabic he speaks. The detainee, a farmer from the outskirts of Fallujah, seems to understand even less.

The capture report contains information from an anonymous source working for U.S. troops. It says the brothers were seen leaving the scene of an explosion. This is typical for capture reports. In Iraq, we joke that the best way not to get arrested is to be seen running toward the scene of an explosion.

I interrogate all five brothers on that first day. I recommend all of them for release. I tell them they should be home in a few days.

Captain Dent meets me in the office and tells me the brothers won't be going home anytime soon. She says they manufacture IEDs. I tell her there was nothing in the capture report. She says, "Just trust that someone knows more than you do." She assigns Sergeant Hoagie to work with me.

Sergeant Hoagie is an Arabic linguist. He is the only other Arabic-speaking interrogator I have met in Iraq. When I meet him he says, "Don't trust the interpreters. You'll get so much more on your own." Hoagie and I interrogate all five brothers again. We start with the oldest and move to the youngest. When the youngest comes into the room Hoagie attacks him. He grabs him by the shirt and pins him up against the wall. Hoagie's Arabic is much better than mine. He's saying something about dogs and liars and brothers and Guantánamo Bay. In February 2004, most Iraqis don't know what's going on inside Abu Ghraib, so they're not afraid to go there. Instead, they fear Guantánamo Bay, so interrogators threaten them with a trip to Cuba.

Hoagie slaps the young brother: one solid open-handed strike to the face. It is loud and violent. In Iraq, I've grabbed detainees, pushed them, shoved them, and tugged at their shirts. But I've never landed a blow on a prisoner of war. I've never punched, kicked, or slapped a detainee. I've never seen anyone else do so, either. But now I have. Now I'm as responsible for it as anyone else.

The young brother is crying. Hoagie sets him down and kneels in front of him. He pats the young man on the arm and uses phrases I don't understand. Hoagie is a better linguist than me. The young brother provides information about the men who store bomb-making materials out in their fields. The brothers monitor the stashes and make deliveries when called upon. They don't set off the devices, but they are often told when and where an attack will take place. Sometimes they go to watch. Americans caught them fleeing from an attack that killed two members of the 82nd. Hoagie writes the report. I just keep thinking about being home in six days.

6.2

In Fallujah, living quarters are cramped. We are housed in an Iraqi military compound that was used by Saddam's most trusted military officers for retreats and conventions. There are pools, fountains, and auditoriums. There is an empty zoo. Soldiers exchange rumors about a striped tiger seen wandering around the compound.

Ferdinand, Jim, and I are shoehorned into a single room. Ferdinand and I do not like Jim. We don't trust him. So we isolate him in the corner. We place our two cots side by side and sleep head to toe. Ferdinand snores. It is a terrible snore. Ferdinand apologizes and explains he has sleep apnea. By the end of the first week, I am seriously sleep deprived.

I conduct at least two interrogations each day. I read through poorly written capture reports that offer little information beyond the detainee's suspected involvement in "anti Coalition activity." Most of the detainees have been turned in by their neighbors, or swept up during search-and-seizure operations. Some simply had too many weapons in their house. But others were caught with mortar tubes in their fields or explosives in their garage.

I search the capture reports for groups of relatives. I learn to use leverage here. I gather the group and interview them all at once. I tell the translators to hold conversations with the detainees. I tell the translators to say something that is funny. Then I laugh. When they realize I speak Arabic, one of the family members will ignore the translator and speak directly to me. He'll say something like "Why have we been arrested?" Or "We support the U.S. troops; we can help you." Or "What right do you have to do this?"

The detainee who speaks up first is the strongest link in the family. I won't waste any time on him. Eventually, others in the group will take their turn to say similar things. Occasionally, one member of the group will be told to keep quiet. They'll interrupt him, or hush him, or put their hands up when he speaks.

I separate the detainees again. I isolate the individual the group tried to keep quiet. I send the rest back to the holding cell. I do paperwork. I play Minesweeper. I return to the isolated detainee. I bring in stacks of paper and manila folders. I tell him the rest of the group has told me about how they fight the Shia. I talk about how they occasionally attack U.S. forces by mistake. I tell him we are not worried about this. We simply want to identify groups that we can work with against the Shia. We just need to know they won't attack U.S. troops anymore.

I want the isolated detainee to admit his family has attacked U.S. forces in the past. I want him to agree to say this with a blindfold on. I want him blindfolded and sitting in front of his other family members when he says this. When it works, there is anger and crying. I pretend not to be bothered by this.

Detainees who have been captured as individuals are more difficult to approach. I learn to estimate their level of influence in Fallujah by the kind of clothes they wear, the way they speak, or the way the other detainees treat them, but in lieu of detailed capture reports it is difficult to know what type of information a detainee may possess. I work to identify detainees who are willing to hold a conversation. Under Saddam Hussein, almost all Iraqis were required to serve in the military. I ask about their experiences and their training. I compare their service with mine. I talk about physical training in the morning and the terrible food served by poorly trained cooks. I talk about annoying leaders or incompetent subordinates. I talk about terrible pay, shoddy equipment, and endless training exercises. I talk about standing outside in the rain, sleeping in the mud, or wearing heavy equipment in the hot afternoon sun. All soldiers have opinions about these things.

The detainees who are willing to talk often reveal a great deal about themselves. They tell me their rank. They talk about the unit they served with and the training exercises they endured. They talk about how much they got paid, about the weapons they learned to fire, the techniques they learned to employ, and the strategies they came to endorse.

As we talk, Tyner, Brent, and Hoagie often conduct interrogations next door. When Tyner is working, there are screams and the sound of plywood chairs and desks being destroyed. I tell my detainees not to worry about these things. I ask them more about the weapons they trained with during their time in service. I ask them if they know anything about explosives or mortar tubes. This makes them nervous. They grow silent. I allow the sounds of Tyner's interrogations to fill the space. I stand behind them, grab their heads with both hands and shove their face away from me. Their hair is slick and greasy. There is more noise from Tyner. The detainees get nervous. I grab the chair and rip it out from underneath them. From the floor, they plead ignorance. I call for Tyner. I leave the room. When I come back, Tyner will say, "Your boy has something to tell you about mortar rounds."

6.3

In mid-February, Captain Dent calls a meeting, at which she tells us that the Army is going to check our credentials. In the meantime, all civilian contractors are prohibited from conducting interrogations. There are rumors about something having gone wrong at Abu Ghraib.

For the next few days, we have nothing to do. I struggle during the downtime. There is time to think about what has been done. A new repeated nightmare arrives. I stand in an empty space with no light. Occasionally someone unseen strikes me. They're gone again. Then someone else from a different angle does the same. The dream seems to last for hours. I wake up expecting someone to strike me. I call this the dark room dream.

After the meeting with Dent, Brent calls his own meeting and tells us there is a major problem brewing at Abu Ghraib. He says not to delete any of our digital photos. There are rumors about soldiers and contractors cooperating with CID at Abu Ghraib. There are rumors about Steven Stefanowicz being arrested. I remind Brent that I am in Fallujah on a temporary basis. I ask him about my position in Baghdad. He tells me to be patient.

Brent covers some administrative details before releasing the group to dinner. He pulls me aside and asks me to walk with him. He says he heard I went to seminary at Princeton. I don't correct him. He says he is Catholic. He says he's not so sure about some of the things that went on at Abu Ghraib, and he's not so sure he did the right thing. He's worried about the hard site. He says he knows I saw the hard site, too. He knows I know what he's talking about. He says he just never expected any of this. I don't have an answer for him.

In February 2004, the Abu Ghraib scandal is beginning to break. The photos of abuse that will alert most Americans to the realities of interrogation in Iraq won't be published for another two months, but in the meantime, the Army is doing its best to get ahead of the growing crisis. The check of our credentials is the first indication that the military intends to begin enforcing rules. This is how the Army often works. It establishes rules, encourages soldiers to ignore them in the name of completing a mission, waits for a reckoning, and then cuts the soldiers off in the name of accountability. The Army is about to cut us off.

We spend a few days in Fallujah, waiting to be reinstated. I receive notice that my credentials have been checked and I'm cleared to return to the interrogation booth. The same is true for Brent. There is no word about Jim. Jim tells Brent that his military interrogation training wasn't official. He says he attended the right schools but never received credit for graduating. He says the Army allowed him to do this so he wouldn't have to give up his job as an analyst. He says the Army wanted an analyst who was knowledgeable about interrogation. Both Brent and I suspect Jim is lying. We don't say this to Jim. Eventually, Jim says he'd rather not conduct interrogations.

None of us hear anything more of the rumors about Abu Ghraib. We go to dinner with Captain Dent and she tells us that we are all expected to be back at work the next morning. On our way back from the dining facility, we come across a crowd of soldiers heading to one of the amphitheaters on the base. It is in a large building with ornate marble columns. Iraqi officers must have gathered here for speeches and presentations. Saddam Hussein likely stood on the stage. Tonight, the Washington Redskins cheerleaders entertain the soldiers of the 82nd Airborne. They play "Hail to the Redskins," followed by a series of patriotic John Philip Sousa marching songs. The finale is Lee Greenwood's "God Bless the USA." Confetti falls from the ceiling as an American flag is unveiled. There is an autograph session with the cheerleaders. It is interrupted by incoming mortars.

The next morning, I interrogate a man named Raad Hussein. He has been badly beaten. His face is swollen. The capture report says that the injuries were sustained when Raad resisted capture. In Bethlehem, I detained men who were resisting arrest. If I had to beat them, I did not beat them in the face. I beat them in the arms and legs, in order to apply the handcuffs.

Hussein says he is the mayor of Fallujah. This makes the interpreter laugh. The interpreter says there are no mayors in Fallujah. Hussein speaks a formal version of Arabic that is easy for me to understand. He also speaks some broken English. I tell the interpreter to leave. I read the capture report. The capture report says Raad Hussein is the mayor of Fallujah. He has been captured because of his suspected involvement in an attack on the police station in the central part of the city. Twenty-three police officers were murdered. The capture report is written by the Army's 5th Special Forces Group. The 5th Special Forces Group often captures detainees in and around Fallujah and turns them over to the 82nd Airborne once they have finished conducting their own interrogations. By the time Raad Hussein sits before me, he has already been thoroughly interrogated.

Hussein tells me that he was attending a meeting with an officer from the 82nd Airborne Division. He says the name of the officer is Drinkwine. Hussein says he was cooperating with the officer and providing information about the attackers. He says the attackers are local extremists looking to impose a strict form of Islam inside Iraq. He says, "It's the Salafis."

I have written a number of interrogation reports in Fallujah about the Salafis. This is what secular Iraqis call their more religiously minded countrymen. Secular Iraqis blame the Salafis for violence in Iraq. In turn, Salafis blame secular Iraqis.

Raad Hussein says that after he left the meeting with Drinkwine he was captured by American Special Forces. He says he knows they were Special Forces because they beat him. He says everyone in Fallujah knows that Special Forces beat people. He also says they drugged him. He tries to show me needle marks, but his skin is too bruised and scarred. I read more of the capture report. There is a page stapled to the back of the report. It says that Raad Hussein has been given a drug. It details his behavior under the influence of this substance. It says he was groggy and unresponsive and the results of the procedure were inconclusive. The report from 5th Special Forces Group concludes that Raad Hussein is of no further intelligence value.

That night, Henson and I gather in a common room where soldiers can watch television on the Armed Forces Network. We are talking about Raad Hussein. We convince each other that he is lying. His whole story is unreasonable. He cannot be the mayor of Fallujah and there cannot be an army officer named Drinkwine. Hussein's English was weak. He must have meant that he was drinking wine with the officer. We laugh about this. The Armed Forces Network is broadcasting PBS. There is a *Frontline* documentary about Iraq. Martin Smith from PBS is traveling throughout the Sunni Triangle to assess the progress of the war. Henson and I watch as he arrives in Fallujah. He talks to Iraqi citizens who criticize the occupation. Then he talks to the mayor of Fallujah. Raad Hussein. Later, Martin Smith interviews an American officer named Lieutenant Colonel Brian Drinkwine. The interview is interrupted by another soldier, who tells Drinkwine that an American helicopter has been shot down.

During the day I catch up on paperwork and read through screening reports about detainees who have yet to be interrogated. In the afternoon a new batch of detainees arrives. Ferdinand asks me to help him with the screenings. These are simple interviews consisting of basic questions. We photograph the detainees, inventory their belongings, and escort them to the detention facility.

Ferdinand and I spend the day together pretending we are police officers again.

At the end of the day, we return to the office and file the completed screening reports. Tyner and Dent are in the office. Dent ordered Tyner to interrogate Raad Hussein after I determined he was of no further intelligence value. Tyner says, "Did you hear about your friend Raad?" Raad Hussein confessed to conspiring with the group responsible for killing the twenty-three police officers in Fallujah. It was likely a power play designed to win the approval of former Baath party elements looking to regain control of the province. Raad found himself in a difficult position. He wanted to secure his job, so he helped murder twenty-three police officers. Tyner cross-referenced Raad's confession with other sources. It's confirmed. Raad is guilty of facilitating the deaths of twenty-three Iraqi police officers.

We pass by the interrogation room where Tyner has been working on Raad Hussein. We haven't heard Tyner scream or throw anything today. The door to the room, a flimsy sheet of plywood, has blown open in the hot desert wind. Inside, Raad Hussein is bound to the Palestinian chair. His hands are tied to his ankles. The chair forces him to lean forward in a crouch, forcing all of his weight onto his thighs. It's as if he's been trapped in the act of kneeling down to pray, his knees frozen just above the floor, his arms pinned below his legs. He is blindfolded. His head has collapsed into his chest. He wheezes and gasps for air. There is a pool of urine at his feet. He moans: too tired to cry, but in too much pain to remain silent.

Henson comes out into the hallway and walks past the room. He covers the side of his face as he walks by and says, "I don't even want to know."

I am silent. This is a sin. I know it as soon as I see it. There will be no atonement for it. In the coming years, I won't have the audacity to seek it. Witnessing a man being tortured in the Palestinian chair requires the witness to either seek justice or cover his face. Like Henson in Fallujah, I'll spend the rest of my life covering my face.

Tyner says he's leaving Raad in the chair for a while, just to see if there's anything else he hasn't shared. I think of the dead police officers in Fallujah. I want to avenge these men, so I tell myself I have an obligation to use aggressive techniques against people like Raad Hussein. I tell myself that Raad is evil and it is necessary to lie to him, necessary to torture him. In a test of my own convictions I say, "He deserves it."

Ferdinand hears me say this. He grabs my shoulder in an aggressive way and says, "Hey, man." I drop my head, close my eyes, and touch my face with my fingertips. Ferdinand says, "I know, me too." We accept the undeniable truth that we are guilty.

Ferdinand and I walk to the dining facility and talk about Raad Hussein. On the way, on an exposed portion of the base, mortars rain down. Ferdinand lifts his arms in the air and pretends he is a baseball player trying to catch a pop fly. He says, "I got it, got it." We both laugh. Ferdinand says, "It would be a mercy killing."

6.4

There is an operations center on base where I can access a classified computer network. I use the computer from time to time to prepare for interrogations. I look at aerial photos of Fallujah and examine pictures of the neighborhoods where the detainees live. I access reports on IED attacks and study information about the types of weapons being used. I find a report about the attack on the police station in Fallujah and in it there are photographs of dead police officers. They rest on the floor, side by side, as if in formation. Some are still dressed in uniform, black pants and a light-blue shirt. Shoulder boards display their rank. Others have been stripped naked, their uniforms taken by insurgents for use in future attacks. Some of the faces show the shock of death, a frozen acknowledgment of the end of life. Other faces are torn open, leaking fluids onto the floor. The police station has large rooms where the officers likely gathered for briefings, smaller rooms that housed higher-ranking individuals, and a front desk where reports were taken. There is blood in every one of these rooms.

I think of the police station in Bethlehem. I think of the patrol room and the front desk and the records room. I think of my friends with bloodied uniforms, or naked, or with holes in their faces. I think I would kill the men responsible.

Ferdinand and I walk to work. We talk about the police stations where we worked and the police officers we worked with. We talk about how difficult the job was and how poorly people treated us. We talk about the impossible job required of Iraqi police officers.

But no matter how hard we try, no matter how much someone like the mayor of Fallujah disgusts us, we cannot justify the Palestinian chair. And as we struggle to justify the chair, we struggle to make sense of everything else we have done. We have been justifying the use of different forms of torture by calling them enhanced techniques and filling out the appropriate paperwork. We have told ourselves all of it has been done in the pursuit of a defensible cause, that it has been done to men like Raad Hussein, and it has been done to men guilty of so much worse. But having seen the Palestinian chair, it's impossible to deny that it has all been wrong.

When we arrive at the office, we agree to take turns in the Palestinian chair. Maybe it's not as bad as we've made it out to be. We experiment with different positions and tell each other what hurts the most. We agree that having your hands secured to the lowest part of the chair puts the most strain on our legs. What begins as a searing burn in the calves and quads evolves into a tearing sensation in the hamstrings and lower back. You sweat, you shake, you can't breathe. It is a violent and frightening pain. It's torture.

Captain Dent arrives to find Ferdinand and me recovering from the chair. She has just come from a briefing with the division commander. He wants better results from the interrogation team. He's not impressed. He may show up in person to observe our interrogations. We'd better be ready.

This is typical for the Army. A lower-ranking officer wants to motivate the troops, so the lower-ranking officer threatens enlisted soldiers with the words of a higher-ranking officer. To hammer home the point, the lower-ranking officer says the higher-ranking officer might show up in person. In truth, the higher-ranking officer has no intention of showing up. And the higher-ranking officer may never actually have said the things attributed to him by the lower-ranking officer, but the tactic has its desired effect. Captain Dent says the division commander wants better results. Captain Dent knows what goes on in the interrogation booths in Fallujah, she knows about stress positions, she knows about slapping detainees, and she knows about the Palestinian chair. Now she says more is expected of us.

6.5

As violence increases throughout Fallujah, the number of detainees at our facility grows. We never expected to have more than a dozen detainees assigned to any one interrogator at a time. There are now more than two hundred in the holding cells. We have fallen behind. We can no longer afford to have interrogators sitting around waiting for one of the two interrogation rooms to become available. Captain Dent breaks us into two shifts. Ferdinand, Henson, and I are assigned to the night shift. She tells us to cancel the day's interrogations and return in the evening. I give the screening reports to Tyner.

Ferdinand, Henson, and I have the rest of the day to prepare for night shift. Ferdinand and I talk about finding new jobs. He has friends who work for DynCorp, a security contractor in Iraq tasked with guarding dignitaries working at the embassy. Ferdinand knows the hiring manager. He says hiring is done by word of mouth. I won't even have to submit a résumé.

6.6

I ask Ferdinand whether he'd consider working for the NSA. We could both move to Maryland. Our wives could meet. He says he doesn't have that type of experience. I tell him it's all about how you write your résumé. At night, instead of conducting interrogations, we sit in the office next to the holding cell and work on his résumé. I write the Iraq section for him:

- Served as subject matter expert for a wide range of security issues in Iraq
- Presented briefings and written assessments to General Officers and high-ranking members of U.S. government
- Responsible for producing accurate and timely assessments of emerging trends in Iraq and acquiring extensive amounts of supporting evidence
- Worked extensively with liaison services from a variety of intelligence and law enforcement agencies
- Conducted interviews of Iraqi security detainees in order to gather information on emerging security threats in the Middle East

Ferdinand says, "You lie like a champ. No wonder you got rejected by seminary."

Ferdinand and I stop conducting interrogations at night. Instead, we sit and talk and make plans for our next job. Ferdinand and I are convinced there is a more honorable way to do war. We'll work a security detail on the streets of Iraq. We'll leave the ugly world of interrogation and return in a more honorable position. We consider starting our own contracting company. Ferdinand has contacts. I do, too. We'd run the company the right way, spend money on the right equipment, provide the right kind of services. It would be an honorable company. It would do impressive things. But we still can't bring ourselves to quit. We still don't want to be seen as the type of people who aren't cut out for doing their part. And so we hang on a little longer.

I send an email to my old hiring manager at the NSA and tell him I'm considering coming home. I pull out old paperwork with names and phone numbers and email addresses. There's a copy of my application to the Princeton Theological Seminary. Ferdinand asks to see it. He reads through the essay about how God doesn't cause suffering and is always working to move us forward. He says I should reapply. The Palestinian chair is sitting in the corner. I say, "I'm pretty sure that ship has sailed."

The next night, there is a note from Captain Dent. She says our lack of work is unacceptable and she expects us to conduct at least five interrogations in order to make up for lost time. I'm concerned about the tone of the note, but Ferdinand tells me to blow it off. He says, "What's she going to do? Fire us?" We spend another night ignoring interrogations. We get another nasty note from Dent. I begin to feel better.

Eventually, we get back in the booth. We bring detainees into the room and ask them questions about the PIRs. None of the detainees answer the questions. We recommend everyone for release. During the day, Dent tracks us down, wakes us up, and demands that we return to work and question detainees until they provide valuable information.

In the booth, Ferdinand pulls out a small flashlight attached to his keychain. It is a small LED set into the shell casing of a .40-caliber bullet. Ferdinand tells me to shine the light in the eyes of the detainee and pretend to scan his brain. Ferdinand stands behind him and makes buzzing noises. The detainee laughs. We laugh, too. We recommend him for release.

On one Saturday night Ferdinand and I talk about church. He is Catholic, but he admits he hasn't been to Mass since coming to Iraq. He doesn't want his family to know this. I tell him I went to chapel at Abu Ghraib a few times, but not since coming to Fallujah. He asks me to hear his confession. I remind him I'm not Catholic. I remind him I was rejected by seminary. He says I'm more than qualified. I remind him I'm Presbyterian. He says, "It's not like I'm ever going to say this shit to a priest."

As I conduct more and more interrogations in Fallujah, my Arabic begins to improve. The dialect becomes more familiar and I find myself better able to communicate with a variety of Iraqi detainees. One evening, however, a detainee arrives who speaks the very formal Modern Standard Arabic. It is the Arabic of DLI. He is well educated and well spoken. He says he is Salafi. He requests permission to lead his fellow detainees in prayer. I allow this. He requests a washbasin filled with clean water. I allow this as well. He asks for his Koran. I deliver it to him.

I identify the men he prays with. I inspect their capture reports. One of the capture reports contains photos of the building from which all the men were taken. It is a small cinder-block building with bars on the windows and doors. The photos from inside depict a collection of sharp knives and blunt instruments. There are tables and chairs with chains and bindings. I've seen buildings like this before. I know a great deal about the Sunni-Shia divide in Iraq. I know the history, the myths, and all the right terms. But the buildings and tables with sharp knives and bars on the windows make all that knowledge meaningless.

In the buildings, one type of Iraqi tortures another type of Iraqi to death. I don't pretend to understand why anymore. Maybe some Iraqis felt called to protect their own type of people. Maybe, at some point, life fell apart for them. Maybe there was a closed door. Maybe they blame this on other types of Iraqis. Maybe they struggle with their own convictions. What remains of one type of Iraqi is deposited on the streets in order to incite fear and encourage compliance in other types of Iraqis.

There are two photographs from outside the cinder-block building. There are three arms and two legs in a pile of damp sand. One photograph shows a dog, lying under a tree, gnawing on the third leg. These detainees belong to one of the barbaric death squads that will bloody Iraq in the years to come.

I wait for the men to finish praying. I return the detainee to the interrogation room and show him the pictures. In Arabic I ask, "Is this what God loves?" He says, "We worship the same God. You are

Christian. I am Muslim. It is the same God." I point to the arms and legs. I point to the sharp tools. He says a word I don't understand. I page through my Arabic dictionary. The word means "strange" or "weird." He repeats it. He says more about us worshiping the same God. I leave to find the translator.

The translator says, "He's talking about fairies." I look confused. The translator says, "Faggots, he's talking about faggots. He knows we hate faggots as much as he does. He's saying they only kill faggots." In English, the detainee says, "Yes, yes, same God, same God." I return him to the holding cell and assign the entire group to Tyner.

In the days to come, I make a concerted effort to select low-priority detainees. Most of them have not been interrogated because no one suspects them of anything. Some detainees are simply rounded up in sweeps and mistakenly sent to the interrogation facility. We get to them when we can and process them for release. I do my best to make sure none of these detainees get assigned to Tyner. The capture reports often say, "Detainee was seen running from the scene of an explosion." I conduct these interrogations on my own. I ask basic background questions while I prepare the paperwork for release. Most of these detainees seem happy to be going home, but after one interrogation, when I get up to leave, one of these detainees cries. He says he does not want to go to Abu Ghraib. In English he says, "Give me food. I have information."

I return with grape juice and a piece of birthday cake from the common room. He devours them and asks for more. I return with more cake and a linguist. He asks for Coca-Cola. I spend the next six hours delivering food while struggling to record all of the information he provides. It is my most productive interrogation in Iraq. When it's over, I have answered a large number of PIRs. I have discovered weapons caches, located a mechanic's shop that builds car bombs, and obtained information on the downing of an American helicopter over Fallujah. The pilot was Kimberly Hampton. She is the first female military pilot to be shot down and killed. I Google her and find she went to school at Presbyterian College.

Ferdinand and I return to the office and process the paperwork.

The day shift arrives before we have finished. Jim isn't conducting interrogations anymore. He works only as an analyst, but he offers to complete our remaining paperwork from the night before and turn it in to Captain Dent. We thank him, and walk home talking about how sometimes Jim can be a good guy.

A day later, we find out that Jim signed his name on our interrogation paperwork. Dent receives a congratulatory note from the commander of the 82nd Airborne. It thanks Jim for his outstanding work. Ferdinand says, "Hey, man, let it go."

As Ferdinand and I recommend more detainees for release, the numbers in the holding cell begin to decline. At night we continue to work on Ferdinand's résumé and talk about finding time to go to chapel. We stand outside the interrogation facility and eat Girl Scout cookies sent by a sixth-grade class from Lexington, Massachusetts. Milk is hard to come by, so we drink boxed Hi-C orange drink we smuggled out of the dining facility. There is a furious growl as a rocket descends from behind. Ferdinand and I buckle at the knees as the rocket overshoots the detention facility and detonates nearby. Its payload lights up the sky. Ferdinand says, "Only a matter of time."

6.7

The detention facility is guarded by a group of military policemen from the Massachusetts National Guard. They make frequent trips to Abu Ghraib and Baghdad in order to transfer the detainees recommended for further interrogation. When we can, we accompany them on these convoys in order to coordinate with the interrogators who will continue the interviews. We also take the opportunity to deliver supplies to CACI personnel who are still stationed at Abu Ghraib.

In March 2004, the 1st Marine Division is deployed to Fallujah in order to relieve the 82nd Airborne Division. The two units spend a month running joint patrols and handing over responsibility for the area. The Marines and soldiers run a joint patrol to Abu Ghraib in order to deliver a group of detainees. There is no room for interrogators. We stay behind and conduct interrogations. The patrol is struck by an IED, injuring two Marines.

A soldier is killed by an IED in Baghdad. Two soldiers are killed by an explosion just outside of Baghdad. A soldier is killed in a convoy in Baqubah. Two National Guard soldiers are killed by an IED in Fallujah. Another soldier is killed by an IED in Fallujah. A National Guard soldier dies when he drives over a land mine. A soldier dies in a bomb blast. Two soldiers die in an attack on their convoy. A soldier is blown up in Tikrit. A soldier dies in a vehicle accident. A soldier drowns in a canal. A National Guard soldier dies in a mortar attack. A soldier is electrocuted in Baqubah. A Marine is killed by an IED. A soldier is killed when his weapon explodes. Another soldier dies in a traffic accident in Fallujah. A soldier is killed in Baghdad. Two soldiers are killed by rocket fire in Fallujah. A soldier is shot and killed in Ramadi. A military policeman is killed in Fallujah. A Marine is killed in Fallujah. A soldier is killed by an explosive device in Baghdad. A Marine is killed west of Baghdad. A soldier is killed by an IED in Ramadi. A Marine is killed in Baghdad. An Army Special Forces soldier is killed. In Habbaniyah, a bomb explodes under a vehicle and kills all five soldiers inside. In San Antonio, at the Alamo Dome, Duke, Oklahoma State, Georgia Tech, and Connecticut qualify for the NCAA Final Four tournament.

April will be worse. Much worse. I no longer feel as though I've missed my war.

6.8

One day in March, a group of detainees arrive at the interrogation facility. Most of them are wounded. We sort them into groups and shove them to the ground when they speak. We clean the blood from the back of the truck and load another group of prisoners who are headed to Abu Ghraib. I head back inside and spend the rest of the night conducting interrogations.

Among the prisoners are a young boy and an old man. They don't know each other, but they both live near an intersection in Fallujah where American troops are frequently ambushed. I bring them both into the room. I stand the old man up in the corner. I sit the young boy down in a chair, but he doesn't understand my directions and keeps trying to stand back up. The boy says he has never seen anyone fire a weapon at American troops. He says no one in his neighborhood knows anything about this. He says he does not know the intersection. He says he has never heard any shooting in Fallujah. He says it must be the Salafis.

As Ferdinand and I have slowed our pace in the interrogation booth, other members of the team like Dent, Brent, and Tyner have taken notice. We've been critiqued for poor performance, and told to work harder. I've grown weary of interrogations, but I'm also embarrassed to be seen as someone who isn't doing his job. Ferdinand tells me to ignore it, but I lack his confidence.

I can find legitimate excuses for letting most prisoners go, and I can make a case to Dent to support most of these decisions. But the young boy's lies are flagrant and glaring. I'm afraid that if someone else interrogates him after I recommend him for release, I'll appear incompetent.

The boy's lies mean nothing. If anything, they demonstrate good character. He isn't afraid of an interrogator. He will not betray his neighborhood. He is someone to trust. I should let him go. The war will not change. None of this will make me a police officer again. But instead of seeing a courageous young boy caught in an impossible situation, I see a threat to my image and my integrity. I've ruined those things on my own, but, like the bad training officers from the Bethlehem Police Department, I assign blame and avoid compassion. I respond in anger.

I rip the plastic chair out from underneath him. I've forgotten about the old man in the corner. When he moves in to help the boy,

I shove him out of the way. He stumbles and his head hits the wall. Thud. The young boy looks up at me from the floor in confusion. He lifts his hands, palms up, and points them at the old man. The sound of the old man's head hitting the wall is like the judge's gavel at the end of a trial. I want to go home.

I return to the office, where Ferdinand and Henson are sorting through screening reports. I say, "I think I may have had enough." Ferdinand says, "Hey, man, no worries. Relax. We'll cover you tonight."

We get mail the next day and there are three letters from Karin. One is from Mexico, where she was attending the wedding of a mutual high school friend. One of the letters has a picture in it, the first picture I've received from Karin while I've been away. She is on the beach, in her bathing suit. There is also a letter from my Presbyterian grandmother. She talks about my grandfather and his service in Europe. And although she uses kind words to compare me to him, she also says she didn't want to see this happen again.

I show the photos to Ferdinand. He shows me photos, too, of his wife and young son on vacation in Arizona. The boy, like Ferdinand, is smiling. He's wearing a T-shirt that says something patriotic about U.S. troops. I think the boy is beautiful.

We head to breakfast and say nothing. Ferdinand and I are spending more and more time together, but we are saying less and less. Others know Ferdinand as the one who always talks, the one who is always holding court, always telling stories, always making people laugh. It's good to be around Ferdinand. He makes you forget where you are. But in Fallujah, Ferdinand grows quiet.

Ferdinand and I no longer hold conversations about whether Brent is a good leader, or whether Dent has any idea what she is doing, or whether Tyner is a war criminal. We don't want to remember shoving old men and questioning young children. We focus on our pancakes and bacon. We steal Hi-C drinks and hide them in our bags. We walk to the building with the free Internet and hit the send/receive button. We head back to our room as the morning heat rises and retreat to our bunks. We sleep through afternoon mortar attacks, then wake in time for dinner. We sit at dinner and say nothing. We steal more drinks. We walk to the slaughterhouse and prepare for the evening. Ferdinand and I come to rely on each other for silence.

We sit outside in the gravel parking lot near the slaughterhouse and wait for shift change. The MPs have adopted a stray dog. I've come to know him well. He chews on my boot. Ferdinand wrestles a stick from his mouth. In a few weeks, the Marines will arrive and take over the base. They'll discover most of the dogs are diseased, so they implement a safety policy and shoot all the dogs.

The next night, when I arrive at the interrogation facility, one of the interpreters pulls me aside and tells me that he overheard the detainees talking to each other in the holding cell. They were saying something about one of the interrogators. He says he thinks they were talking about me. He says he thinks he heard the word "Satan."

The next day I interrogate a former major in the Republican Guard's Hammurabi Division. The major speaks English. He claims innocence. I fill out the paperwork that will send him to Abu Ghraib. At the end of the interview, I ask him what he and other detainees talk about inside the detention facility. I ask about the word "Satan." He talks about the Salafis and says these are the men we should both be fighting. He tells me that he protects the younger detainees from these men. He says the Salafis are dirty and stupid. He says they try to hold religious services inside the holding cells. They make the men pray and bother those who don't have beards. He offers to help interrogate the Salafis. I ask the major whether the detainees talk about the interrogators. He says they have names for each of us. There is the black Satan, the white Satan, and the fat one. I ask him what they call me. He says, "You, the one who speaks fus-ha, the quiet one, the kind one. Everyone wants to be assigned to you."

I feel good about this, which is absurd. A prisoner would be foolish to tell me the truth, to tell me that his comrades hate me, think of me as subhuman, want to kill me in my sleep. He is smart to compliment me. I am dumb to believe it. But my insecurity has no limits, so I accept him at his word, pretend that my trespasses have been less than those of my colleagues, and take pride in thinking that I am not one of the "Satans." It's nice to think of myself as a light amidst the darkness.

I've abused prisoners in Fallujah and in Abu Ghraib. I have pulled chairs out from underneath young boys. I shoved an old man into a wall. I was silent in the face of the Palestinian chair. I failed to protect the men in my care. I tortured them. And now I believe they like me.

6.9

The next night, Brent meets me at shift change to inform me that I'm being transferred back to Baghdad. My new team members have arrived and it is time for me to start working in my assigned position. He says it will be important work. I read through the daily report and listen to the brief from Captain Dent. As the day shift prepares to leave, Brent asks me to spend some time that evening with one of his detainees. He is utilizing sleep deprivation. I am to wake the detainee up at random times. Every hour is fine, but don't make it too consistent. And strip him, too. We're not looking to induce exposure; just take his coat long enough to cool him down. The key is to keep him awake.

The night shift leaves. I read reports on the detainees I'll be interrogating. I grab a Hi-C drink and Girl Scout cookies from the common room and spend some time outside listening to the outgoing rounds from the artillery units stationed on base. The rounds detonate in the distance. I don't think about sleep deprivation. I think about following Brent's instructions. It's not my interrogation. It's not my sin. At one a.m., I awaken the detainee. He smells. He is shaking. I make him stand up and I take his coat. Underneath, he is naked. He cries.

I return the coat, turn off the light, and let him sleep. I hope there is a way back.

7

In Baghdad, I run. I run past the canals that feed the artificial lakes of Saddam Hussein's presidential retreat. The large palaces were all damaged during the initial days of the invasion, but the smaller villas and vacation homes remain largely intact. A variety of American military units have set up their headquarters in the abandoned structures. The roofs are covered in an array of antennas and sandbags. The sun rises and begins to heat the day. I turn around and head back to CACIville. I am passed by armored Humvees and an assortment of tracked vehicles. Mortar rounds strike an empty field. I keep pace with a group of soldiers running in formation.

Brent was wrong. My new team members have not arrived. It will be another week. CACI leaders give me a certificate of appreciation for my voluntary work at Abu Ghraib and Fallujah. I also get a plastic CACI coffee mug and a $10 certificate to spend at the post exchange. I buy Gatorade and Doritos. I'm told to be patient and enjoy the time off. I'm assigned my own room in an old Iraqi army barracks. The room has a door with a lock. It is the first time I've been inside a locked room since arriving in Iraq. I go to the room and lock the door.

Ferdinand and I spent our last night together talking about sleep deprivation. It was the first time I remember using the word "torture" in a conversation in Iraq. We both knew the Palestinian chair was torture, but I don't remember saying it. But sleep deprivation can be described no other way.

That evening, I eventually left the detainee in the room and allowed him to sleep for the rest of the night. When Brent arrived the next morning, I said, "I don't know, I don't know what to tell you." Brent apologized. He said, "Yeah, you know, I don't think I want to do it anymore, either."

I write a letter to Karin from the locked room in Baghdad. It is April. My midtour vacation is in May. I write to Karin about traveling in Europe or swimming at a beach in the Maldives, about airplane flights, good food, and bathing suits. I write that I am happy to be gone from Fallujah. I write about my morning runs on Camp Victory. I write about the canals and the artificial lakes. I ask her to send me a new batch of clothes. I need hot-weather shirts. I do not write about sleep deprivation. I do not write about waking up at night to make sure my door is locked.

Bill Jenkins, my new team leader, soon arrives in Iraq. He is a former Army warrant officer with more than twenty years' experience in the intelligence community. I help him with his gear and give him a tour of the complex. He talks about CACI's hiring process and about the deployment process at Fort Bliss. He says, "Worst I've ever seen." He talks about the other CACI employees on his flight. He suspects the vast majority of them forged their résumés. He wonders whether any of them have actually served in military intelligence. He says, "Bottom of the barrel."

Bill and I talk about our new team and the details of our assignment. We are tasked with creating a five-member unit that will support military counterintelligence units and provide expert analysis of emerging trends inside Iraq while offering critical assessments of evolving insurgent capabilities and motivations. I tell Bill I'm not qualified to do this. I tell him I was an Arabic linguist trained to do long-range reconnaissance and that I was a police officer. I say the only emerging trend is more incoming mortars and more angry Iraqis. Bill says, "Just pretend you know what you're doing."

7.1

Easter arrives. The nightmares have become more frequent. On Easter morning, I go for a run on Camp Victory. I explore a new portion of the base where the Army's 1st Cavalry Division is setting up. A large artificial hill rises out of the empty fields. This is where the workers piled the dirt to dig out the canals and lakes for Saddam's palaces. Everyone says this is where Saddam Hussein buried the chemical weapons. From the top of the hill I can see the buildings and minarets of Baghdad. I hear the Muslim call to prayer and think about Sunday services at the First Presbyterian Church. I remember an organ prelude accompanied by the Philadelphia Brass, the choir processing down the aisle and singing "Jesus Christ Is Risen Today." The "Hallelujah Chorus" from Handel's *Messiah*. In high school, I used to attend all four Easter services before getting French-kissed in the church parking lot.

A large formation of soldiers from the 1st Cav Division reaches the top of the hill. They stop for push-ups and sit-ups. The sergeant berates the stragglers who are still making their way up the hill. His profanity is interrupted by incoming mortar rounds. We scatter over the sides of the hill and make our way back down to lower ground. I sit with other soldiers in a bunker made of large cement highway dividers. An officer says, "They watch from the minarets. Fucking assholes call artillery on Easter Sunday from a fucking mosque."

CACI organizes training sessions for newly arrived employees. They ask me to teach Arabic. I sit in a classroom while another employee gives a PowerPoint presentation on the difference between Sunni and Shia. I listen to a speech about the Baath party. There is a class on terrorism. I stand up front and recite basic Arabic greetings. When it's over, one of the employees organizes everyone into teams. He tells me to say words in Arabic and then call on the teams to see who was paying attention. He uses a whiteboard to keep score. Bill gets up to leave and tells me to come with him. He says, "I didn't come to Iraq to play games."

Bill commandeers a vehicle and tells me to show him the airport.

We drive to Baghdad International and visit the duty-free shop. We buy whiskey and Cuban cigars. We return to our room and spend the rest of Easter Sunday getting drunk. I had access to alcohol in Fallujah, but I rarely drank. I was too busy, and when I wasn't busy, I was talking with Ferdinand. There were too many interrogations to conduct. In Baghdad, there is nothing for us to do yet, so I stay drunk for a week. The alcohol dulls the nightmares. Bill watches over me.

7.2

On April 18, I go back to work. Bill decides that we do not need a five-man team to do the assigned job. He says, "The last thing we need are more CACI guys." The two of us are attached to an Army intelligence unit tasked with gathering information on the Iraqi workers who enter Camp Victory during the day. They paint the walls, fix the roads, gather the trash, and suck the shit out of the portable toilets. The jobs are highly sought after by Iraqi citizens. The pay is better than anything they can find in Baghdad. Iraqis form long lines at the checkpoints, hoping to land day jobs on Camp Victory.

I arrive at the main gate in the mornings and make my way through long lines of Iraqi citizens. The U.S. military suspects that members of a number of insurgent groups are mixing with the workers in order to gather information about the troops on base. They also suspect they are recording the locations of important buildings in order to facilitate more accurate mortar fire.

I walk among the Iraqis and practice my Arabic. They are eager to speak with someone who knows the language. They think I am someone with influence, so many tell me about their brothers who were taken by American troops, or their fathers who never came home, or their cousins who disappeared last month, or their uncles arrested by the Iraqi police. They complain about the checkpoints that keep them from visiting relatives or the military convoys that make them late for work. They want to know why their child's school was destroyed and who will be rebuilding it.

I listen to the stories and field the complaints. I pretend to write names down in my notebook and promise to report back when I have more information. More and more Iraqis come to see me and make the same complaints. I make the same assurances. An older man holds my hand and guides me through the crowd. He introduces me to his teenage sons. One of them wears a shirt with the word "Jesus" printed on the front. He shows me the cross he is wearing around his neck, then points at me, then back at himself. He says, "Christian." They are Chaldean Christians, like Tariq Aziz, the deputy prime minister under Saddam Hussein. Coalition forces arrested Tariq Aziz not long after the invasion, and he is a detainee in an American prison in Iraq.

The old man sits down with me and says something about Abu Ghraib. I struggle with the Arabic, with his accent. I continue to hear the name "Abu Ghraib." I make out other words, too. He is speaking in the second person. He is speaking about me. He says I interrogated him at Abu Ghraib.

I return to the main gate and spend the better part of the afternoon helping American soldiers inspect Iraqi vehicles entering the base. I translate for the drivers and check worker identification cards. The platoon sergeant arrives, and I tell him about meeting the old man from Abu Ghraib. He says, "Former detainees can't get on base. We need to take him out of the line."

I ride back outside the gate with the platoon sergeant and track down the old Christian man and his sons. I wave him over to the vehicle. He thinks I've orchestrated a job for him, so he thanks me. We drive the old man onto Camp Victory and place him in a small room. When I enter the room, he smiles. I tell him he's permanently banned from working on Camp Victory.

7.3

A few days later, I see Ferdinand again. He, Brent, and Henson have
made the trip from Fallujah in order to deliver Michael Bagdasarov
to Camp Victory. Bagdasarov was my replacement in Fallujah. He
arrived a few days after I left. Abu Ghraib was difficult for him.
Fallujah was worse. Ferdinand tells me Bagdasarov's morale deteriorated quickly. He argued with Captain Dent about release forms, he
argued with Brent about working on the night shift, and he argued
with Tyner about the legality of the Palestinian chair.

After a particularly difficult day in Fallujah, Bagdasarov had a
confrontation with a Marine officer at the dining facility. Bagdasarov
was wearing a baseball cap. The officer approached him and told
him to remove it. Bagdasarov refused. An argument ensued. Bagdasarov lost his temper, stood up, and pointed his finger in the Marine
officer's face. Bagdasarov was detained and taken to a holding cell.
It took Brent all day to retrieve him. When he did, the Marines told
Brent to take him back to Baghdad.

I spend the afternoon with Ferdinand, helping him resupply for
his return to Fallujah. We visit the post exchange and the duty-free
shop at the airport. I tell him he should stay in Baghdad. He tells me
to come back to Fallujah. We both agree we won't be with CACI
much longer. I tell Ferdinand I'm still having trouble with the sleep-
deprivation thing. He tells me Brent is using the technique more and
more. Ferdinand says, "Hey, man, maybe it's time to say something."
I tell Ferdinand I'm behind him. He says, "No, not me, you. You're
the one who needs to say something. You're the priest."

In late April 2004, *60 Minutes* broadcasts the photographs of
detainees at Abu Ghraib. Some of the activities in the photographs
are familiar to me. Others are not. But I am not shocked. Neither is
anyone else who served at Abu Ghraib. Instead, we are shocked by
the performance of the men who stand behind microphones and say
things like "bad apples" and "Animal House on night shift."

Ferdinand and I stop talking about Abu Ghraib, Fallujah, and
sleep deprivation. We don't want to be identified as the bad apples

or the guys in the Animal House. We don't want to be hung out to dry. We are guilty, but we don't want to go to jail. Instead, we talk about going home, finding new jobs, and coming back to Iraq. We tell each other we'll get it right next time. We'll put our lives on the line. We'll do it the honorable way. I don't know how, but we still believe one exists.

7.4

The next morning, I bring Bagdasarov with me to the front gate. Bill is happy to have an experienced interrogator on the team and allows us to work together. I show Bagdasarov the lines of Iraqi workers and walk him out into the crowd. As we turn and head back toward the base, I see the Christian man from Abu Ghraib with his sons. They're standing in line again, desperate to get back on base for the higher wage. I greet them and let them through.

Bagdasarov and I spend the week sorting through Iraqi workers at the front gate. I wander through the crowds and pretend to understand what the Iraqis are saying to me. The older men keep their distance. The teenagers approach me and say, "New York Yankees." A middle-aged man hands me a piece of paper. I can't read the handwriting. I return to the front gate and wait for the man to be processed through. When he enters, I have soldiers separate him as though he is being detained. I meet with him in a holding room, where I'm joined by a translator. The Iraqi man asks for help. He heard about what I did for Joseph, the old Chaldean Christian from Abu Ghraib. He heard I let him back on base. Joseph told the man to come to me for help.

The man's brother has been arrested by Iraqi police in Baghdad. He says Iraqi police are arresting Christians. He says his brother needs medicine but the Iraqi police will not allow him to deliver it. He asks me to have his brother transferred to U.S. authorities, who will treat him better. I tell him I can't do this. The man cries. I tell him I'll do my best.

I spend the rest of the day and evening buried in my Arabic dictionary. I use paper with an official letterhead from the military intelligence unit. I dig through my old language resources and cut and paste from a variety of formal letters and edicts. I identify myself as an employee of the U.S. government and mention that I work in intelligence. For "intelligence," I use the word *mukhabarat*. In Arabic, this is a powerful word, something akin to Stasi, Gestapo, or KGB. I work hard to produce a professional-looking letter written in Arabic. The next day I deliver the letter to the Iraqi man and tell him this is the best I can do.

The next day he shouts to me as I wander through the crowds at the front gate. His brother is with him. Many other family members are there as well. They surround me and dance. I am hugged and kissed. The letter was delivered to the Iraqi police. The supervising officer arrived within minutes. The brother was released immediately. The police apologized to the family. They offered the family a payment as compensation. I never fully understand how or if the letter made a difference. I don't understand why the Iraqi police would have acted so quickly. I don't understand how I could have played any role in an Iraqi legal issue. I know only that Iraqis thanked me for releasing a man from prison.

7.5

Bagdasarov and I return from work one evening to find John Blee waiting for us in our room. He has quit his job with CACI. He's the first among our original five to do so. He is back in Baghdad to catch a flight home. We take him to the hamburger bar at the dining facility. Blee was the most optimistic member of our group, but Mosul changed that. He doesn't seem young anymore. He is angry and unpleasant. He says, "I don't fucking care." He says this a lot. He says it when we ask him about losing the salary, or about his résumé, or his professional reputation. He says it when we ask him what he'll do next. He says it when we ask him about his wife.

Blee tells terrible stories about Mosul. The stories are about people doing things that are unprofessional, immoral, and illegal. He says some of the guys are doing something with water. I tell Blee about sleep deprivation in Fallujah. Blee looks at me in a pathetic way. He shrugs, laughs, and says, "That's it? That's all? Are you fucking serious?" Later, in Washington, D.C., when I cooperate with the Department of Justice, I'll be asked to identify other CACI personnel with information about what went on in Iraq. I'll tell them to talk to John Blee. After Iraq, Blee and I exchange emails. But after my interview with the Department of Justice, I never hear from John Blee again. I don't know if he ever told anyone else about Mosul.

Bagdasarov says we should all quit. Blee agrees and encourages me to join them on the flight to Kuwait. But I tell both of them to reconsider. I tell them about my six-day plan. Just last another six days. Then another. I figure out how much money we make in six days. I tell them not to underestimate the value of that money. This opportunity won't come again. Blee only repeats, "I don't fucking care." We drive Blee to the airfield the next morning and help him sign up for a flight out of Iraq. After we say good-bye, I think it will be hard to last another six days. Bagdasarov and I report to the front gate for work.

7.6

A few days later, I conduct my final interrogation as a CACI employee. A U.S. soldier witnessed a fight between two groups of Iraqis waiting to enter the base. One man was seen giving orders and directing others in one of the groups. When questioned, he denied involvement. He and the other participants in the fight are waiting for me in holding rooms.

Bagdasarov and I know the man well. We call him the fat man. While he is never the first to arrive in the morning, he is always first in line. None of the other Iraqis ever confront him when he jumps the line. He is funny, talkative, and bald. He knows enough English to be friendly. He organizes the other workers and keeps them in line. He makes fun of the Iraqis who kneel down to pray. He calls them terrorists. He is well dressed. He offers to bring us food and alcohol from Baghdad. He shows us pictures of his family and talks about his two young sons. He shows us pornography. He salutes me and calls me captain. He helps me with my Arabic. I like him.

The participants in the fight are scratched and bruised. Their clothes are disheveled and dirty from wrestling on the ground. The fat man is uninjured. His collared shirt remains clean and tucked in. In Arabic he says "Captain, Captain, it is the terrorists, we fight the terrorists for you."

I spend the day questioning everyone in the group. There are no stress positions. There is no yelling. I do not repeat my questions, or ask them in different ways. I do not pretend to know everything. I do not blindfold the men or secure them to the floor. I do not ask them to repeat answers. I do not attempt to poke holes in their stories. I do not attempt to confuse, intimidate, or mislead. I make no effort to confront the lies. I make no effort to scare anyone.

I write a detailed report of the incident. I write that the fat man is a former high-ranking member of the Baath party. I write that he controls the line of Iraqi workers outside the gate. He ensures that Sunnis are hired first. Some of his former subordinates in the army serve as his bodyguards. They still take orders from the fat man. He was probably a captain. Possibly a major or colonel. His bodyguards intimidate the workers who question his authority. They instigated the physical assault when a group of Shias attempted to move up in the line. All of them should be banned from working on U.S. bases. I confiscate their Coalition identification cards and usher them off Camp Victory.

This is the interrogator I should have been. I could have left Iraq with my soul intact. It is too late for that.

7.7

In the late mornings, after having made my rounds outside the gate, I return to Camp Victory and climb the watchtower that overlooks the vehicle inspection area. The perch affords me a good view. I watch as the remaining workers, mostly Shia, wait in hopes of landing one of the last jobs on base for the day. Many give up and wander in groups back toward the cluster of taxis that will return them to Baghdad. I stare out at the minarets of a nearby mosque where loudspeakers play the call to prayer and spotters call in insurgent mortar fire.

Today there is a rocket attack. The rockets disturb me most. They growl and scream. Just before impact, there is silence. Then flame and noise. One lands nearby. We watch the mushroom cloud rise. I descend the tower and check in with Bill. We report no casualties at the front gate.

The next day I arrive at the front gate by seven a.m. I drink coffee and eat the miniature boxes of cereal I've stolen from the dining facility. I like the Apple Jacks best. I have time to relax before the majority of workers begin to line up. I sit on the ground and rest against the HESCO barriers. Sometimes I think about praying, but I don't.

The sergeant in charge of the morning shift approaches and says there is a disturbance at the gate. I save the Apple Jacks for later. I ride in his vehicle past the heavily armed control points and out to the final barriers where I usually start my rounds. There are two men waiting for us. There are women behind them. These are the first women I have seen at the front gate of Camp Victory.

There are no translators this morning: they have been sent out on another mission. I am the only linguist. The men hold up pictures of their sons. I recognize them: Thaer and Walid, two boys who secured full-time positions on Camp Victory with the help of the fat man. They don't stand in line like the others. They are picked up every morning by a U.S. Navy unit that employs them as general contractors. Thaer and Walid failed to come home last night. They are missing.

I assume the two boys were picked up by one of the security units on Camp Victory. Iraqi workers are often detained for a variety of reasons, questioned, held overnight, and then released the next morning. I leave the families outside the gate and make the necessary phone calls but there are no reports of Iraqis being detained within the last forty-eight hours. A lieutenant on the other end of the line mentions yesterday's rocket attack. There were casualties. Some of them were Iraqi. Check with the morgue.

The morgue is located next to the health clinic where soldiers are treated for sickness and non-combat-related injuries. There is a body waiting for me there. I don't know whether it is Thaer or Walid. The body is stored in a military ambulance. The heat of the day is beginning to envelop Iraq. The ambulance isn't running, so there's been no air-conditioning in the vehicle. Everything inside the ambulance is beginning to bake. When I ask for assistance, I'm told to stand in line like all the others. When I mention the body in the ambulance, I'm told to stand in line like all the others. When I tell them the family of the body is waiting at the front gate, I'm told to wait in line like all the others. All the others are soldiers and U.S. civilians standing in line waiting to see the doctor. They have sore throats, runny noses, and diarrhea.

I abandon the line and head toward the ambulance. Three Army officers are taking a break nearby. One of the officers who was on duty during the rocket attack tells me that both boys were struck by a rocket during the attack. The boy in the ambulance died of his wounds. The other boy was taken somewhere else, but he doesn't know where. I tell him he needs to identify the body in order to notify the family. He says, "Be my guest."

One of the officers, a young lieutenant, reminds me of John Blee. He offers to help. The two of us climb into the back of the ambulance in order to identify the body. The lieutenant hands me a pair of surgical gloves and says, "This won't be pretty."

I unzip the body bag. There is a cascade of images. It appears all at once, but I remember it as individual pictures. The forehead leads to a face, then a mouth, then chin, neck, shoulder, arm, part of a chest, and a space for the abdomen. I know this boy but I don't know the thing in the bag. The thing in the bag has a terrible smell. The lieutenant says, "Nothing smells like burnt people."

I sift through the body's clothing. I invade pockets and peel back the garments. The lieutenant says, "Whoa, no, no, those aren't his clothes, brother." I roll his skin back onto his legs. His penis is gone, cut to shreds by the shrapnel that likely removed most of his stomach. He did not die right away. His face shows the suffering. I don't know how long. It was long enough for him to feel something terrible.

I have opened the bag just below the body's waist. There is no ID card. The lieutenant helps me roll the body on its side in order to check the back pockets. Underneath, fluids have pooled. I accidentally lean up against the bag and create a channel for the fluids to flow. They drip onto my shoes and soak into the dirt on the floor. This will be the source of the liquid nightmares.

There is still no ID card. I open the bag the entire way. The body is fully exposed. The stench is angry. One of the feet is missing. In its place is a plastic bag with personal belongings and identification papers. The ID card says it is Thaer.

Bill is waiting for me at the front gate. He says he has word from CACI leadership. He says they've told me to "separate myself from this thing." The Army will escort the families off the base. Let them give the notifications. They'll take care of the body. They'll find out where the other boy is. I hand the plastic bag to an Army sergeant and tell him the family will have to identify the body.

There are still no linguists at the front gate so the sergeant asks me to talk to the families. The families are waiting in one of the interrogation rooms. Plastic chairs have been brought in for the women. Someone has served them Coke and Pop-Tarts, the blueberry ones with frosting.

In Arabic I say, "There is a problem, one son has died, and one son is still alive." I ask the fathers to come outside. I tell them that Thaer is dead but Walid is still alive. Walid's father cries. Thaer's father doesn't react. I decide then not to separate myself from this thing until it is finished. I escort the two fathers to the field ambulance. I speak with Thaer's father. In Arabic I say, "This will be difficult. Do you understand me?" Thaer's father follows me inside the ambulance. The lieutenant joins us. I unzip the bag to the same cascade of images. The father says, "No, this is Walid."

The ID cards were switched. Thaer survived the attack. Walid is dead. Walid's father is standing in the shade, waiting to console Thaer's father. I deliver the bad news. Walid's father stops crying. I put my hand on him and tell him it's not necessary to identify the body, but he insists on seeing Walid. We go back to the ambulance, back to the smell, back to the bag, and back to the crescendo of images. When Walid's father starts to cry, I close the bag and take him back to the shade where Thaer's father waits to comfort him. I leave the two men alone and sit down in the shade next to the lieutenant. The lieutenant puts his hand on top of my head and says, "You should have been a chaplain."

The ambulance arrives with Walid's body. I instruct the driver to take the body out through the checkpoints where the family will take custody. The driver tells me he isn't allowed to do that. The ambulance has no armor. He isn't permitted to drive past the interior security gates. This is as far as he can go. The family will have to carry the body through the checkpoints. This is a distance of 150 yards.

A sergeant calls me over and hands me a mobile phone. It is a public affairs officer from the Green Zone, the highly fortified American complex in the center of Baghdad. The public affairs officer tells me that an Iraqi citizen just died during surgery. Apparently he was wounded during a rocket attack on Camp Victory. They airlifted him to the trauma center in the Green Zone. They believe his name is Walid. His family needs to come to the Green Zone to retrieve the body. I say, "No, it's Thaer."

I deliver another death notification in Arabic. Then I retrieve a CACI vehicle and pull it up alongside the ambulance. I hoist the body bag onto my shoulder. Walid falls apart. I'm not sure whether he becomes two pieces or just melts into jelly. It's like carrying a bag of water full of sticks and stones. I put the bag in the vehicle and drive the two fathers out past the front gate. A large crowd has gathered on the main road. There is a minivan with a coffin on the roof. The crowd surrounds my vehicle and takes the bag full of Walid from the back. Walid's father holds my hand and walks with me to the minivan. He kisses me on my cheek, then drives away. Thaer's father does the same. He goes on his way to retrieve what's left of his son.

I return to the front gate and go back to work. I translate for a Jordanian worker who has lost his identification papers. I meet a tribal sheik who says the members of his tribe can provide construction services for all of Camp Victory. I process Iraqis who are working on Camp Victory for the first time. I sit in the CACI vehicle and listen to the Armed Forces Network. They play the Black Eyed Peas. Bill takes me to the Bob Hope Dining Facility for dinner and I stand in line at the hamburger bar. That night we smoke cigars and drink. When I head for bed, Bill says, "Take tomorrow off."

7.8

On Camp Victory, there is Morale, Welfare and Recreation (MWR), rooms set aside where soldiers can relax and recharge. It is almost always empty. Bill drops me off at MWR on his way to the front gate and tells me to "hang out for a while." There are sofas, a large screen TV, a collection of books and magazines, and an enormous supply of Girl Scout cookies. There will be many questions about the Iraq war. Some of these questions will concern the general public's detachment and general lack of involvement in the war effort. But the Girl Scouts are beyond reproach. They deliver a nearly endless supply of their signature product. Girl Scout councils and troops from across the nation have banded together to supply troops in Iraq with crates full of Caramel deLites and Thin Mints.

I find a recliner in the corner, commandeer a box of cookies, and read *Maxim* magazine. I stare at Paris Hilton in white underwear.

There are clean portable toilets just outside. A clean portable toilet is a good place to take Paris Hilton. When I return, a group of soldiers is setting up an Xbox. They play a violent game. The television is split into four screens. Each player hunts the other. One player in particular dominates the others, who quickly grow angry. They say, "Fuck you," a lot. They say, "That's fucking bullshit," or "You fucking shit," or "Go fuck yourself." Eventually they start tossing things around the room.

A chaplain enters. I'm still reading *Maxim* magazine. He asks the other men to quiet down and watch their language. There is a church service down the hall. It's Sunday. I'd forgotten. He says, "All of you are welcome." He looks at me. He says, "Even contractors." No one accepts his offer. The other soldiers agree to be quiet. When he leaves, they return to the game. The one player continues to dominate. The others say, "Fuck you," in hushed voices. I go back to tits and Thin Mints.

7.9

I find a way not to quit my job in Iraq, which means I find a way not to ask why I'm still here. I'm a civilian in Iraq, but I find the mind-set of a soldier nearly impossible to give up. Soldiers don't ask questions. They just keep going. It's the only identity I feel I have anymore.

In the meantime, Bagdasarov takes good care of me. Bill does, too. I perform terribly at work. I stop filling out paperwork, and I spend most of my time inside the vehicle listening to the radio. I fall asleep in the front seat. Bill never tells me to get back to work.

There are new nightmares, terrible ones. Pools of sickly fluid dart around the room and nip at my heels. I'm restricted to short quick movements. I can't leave the room. Eventually I climb on top of something, but the liquid follows me there, too.

I write emails to Karin about our itinerary in the Maldives. We've decided to spend my midtour vacation there. I need to stay out of the United States in order to maintain my tax-free status. We'll spend a week on the beach. The trip will be expensive, but I'm making good money. I've pocketed more than $40,000 since January. Karin likes these emails, because they give her purpose. She likes to help me with administrative details and schedules. She likes paperwork and keeping records. She doesn't have to tell me what she thinks about Iraq, or what she thinks about interrogation, or what she thinks about the Abu Ghraib scandal. We never communicate about these things. We communicate about tax-free status, airline tickets, and packing lists.

7.10

A few days after carrying the body bag full of Walid, I send an email to CACI asking for a $50,000 raise. I write that I was hired as an interrogator but I'm also doing the job of a linguist. I write that there are no other CACI employees with my skill set. The email is confrontational, angry, and unprofessional. It still feels wrong to quit, so I'm trying to get fired instead. When I'm not fired, I surrender. I terminate my contract with CACI. When I tell Bagdasarov, he quits, too.

The next day, Ferdinand arrives in Baghdad. He quit in Fallujah. He hitched a ride back to Baghdad with an Army convoy. He hasn't told anyone from CACI. He's heading home on his own. He doesn't care what anyone from CACI thinks.

I'm glad to see Ferdinand. He's funny again. He tells good stories and helps me forget where I am. I'm glad we're going home together. He has another job lined up with DynCorp, where he'll work as a security contractor protecting VIPs in Iraq. He has all the phone numbers and contact information of the people I need to call. They've heard about me and are willing to bring me on. I'll need to attend a short training class in Arizona, qualify on weapons, and then deploy with the team at the end of the summer. When I ask Ferdinand about the NSA, he says, "Hook me up!" I agree to walk him through the hiring process when we get home.

I feel bad about leaving Bill. He was a good team leader. I think things might have been different if there had been leaders at Abu Ghraib like Bill. We go to dinner one last time at the hamburger bar and talk about our time outside the front gate. We do not talk about Walid or Thaer. We agree to reconnect back home to drink and smoke.

8

Ferdinand, Bagdasarov, and I sit in the terminal in Baghdad waiting for a flight out of Iraq and complaining about CACI. We haven't completed our contract term, so CACI is not obligated to pay for our trip home. I'm given a one-way ticket to Fort Bliss, where I'll be required to turn in my gear and pay for my own transportation back to Bethlehem. CACI threatens to withhold pay for any gear that isn't properly returned. Once we finish out-processing at Fort Bliss, we're on our own. Ferdinand, who has worked for contracting companies in Bosnia, says he's never heard of a company operating this way before. He says it is bullshit and he says CACI can keep his final paycheck and shove it up their ass. He tosses his gear in the trash and tells us to do the same. He says, "They're just going to toss it when you get back to Fort Bliss."

In Kuwait, Ferdinand gets in touch with an old friend who works as a supply contractor in Kuwait City. He picks us up from the American airbase and drives us to the mall. We eat mozzarella sticks at TGI Fridays, surrounded by young military-age Kuwaitis who flirt with German girls from a high school tour group. Ferdinand and I ride the escalator in the mall. There are cell phones, sunglasses, and a Starbucks. We spend the night at an apartment complex with a pool and a Jacuzzi.

Ferdinand's friend offers to take care of our travel plans back to the United States. He tells us to take our CACI gear out back and leave it in the Dumpster. It will be cheaper for me to fly straight home to Pennsylvania than to buy a domestic ticket from Texas. I decline the offer.

Ferdinand drives us back to the airbase. We sit at the food court. Even though there's Burger King, KFC, and Pizza Hut, Ferdinand insists we order sandwiches from Subway. He's lost thirty pounds since Abu Ghraib. In Fallujah, he and another contractor went on the Atkins diet. They made a wager about who could last the longest. The loser had to shave his head, and Ferdinand lost. His thick black hair is growing back now. He keeps it short. He is trim and muscular, handsome. He looks like a bodyguard.

I don't remember much from that last day in the food court. I will miss Ferdinand.

8.1

Bagdasarov and I fly to London. I buy a Toblerone and Orangina. We fly to Chicago. I buy popcorn. We fly to Texas. We turn in our gear. The man at supply inspects our gear before tossing it in a large bin labeled "Recycle." Bagdasarov asks him about the bin. The man says the gear is out of date. It will either be destroyed or sold to a surplus store. He says, "Some homeless guy will get it."

Bagdasarov and I go out to dinner, watch a basketball game, and eat more mozzarella sticks. We say little. We return to Fort Bliss to check out and walk back through the processing areas where new contractors are preparing for deployment to Iraq. Michelle Fields is briefing a new group of CACI employees. We stand nearby and listen to what she has to say. She tells them body armor and weapons will be issued in Kuwait. She says they'll have the best armor available, and likely be issued M4s, though some employees still have M16s. Armored vehicles will be waiting for them in Baghdad. She says, "You'll have everything you need." When she finishes, she hands out CACI tote bags filled with T-shirts and mouse pads.

I rent a car and take Bagdasarov to the airport. We agree to meet in Baltimore soon. Beer and soft-shell crabs.

I still haven't called Karin. We've exchanged emails about the logistics of coming home and canceling the trip to the Maldives, but we haven't had an actual conversation since Fallujah. I could be back in Bethlehem in time for dinner, but I'm not ready to go home. Instead, I email Karin telling her I'm going to take the train. I write that it's something I've always wanted to do. It will take three days.

I drive to Albuquerque to catch Amtrak's Southwest Chief. On the way, I cross New Mexico's Gila National Forest. Somewhere along Route 180, I'm pulled over by a reservation police officer. He issues me a ticket for doing forty-five miles per hour in a thirty-five-mile-per-hour zone, and I'm consumed by something terrible. I tell the police officer to go fuck himself. As he walks back to his patrol car, I get out of my vehicle and tell him he's a lousy police officer. I wait for him to order me back inside, but he doesn't. I approach his vehicle. I shout more things. As he pulls away, I slap the passenger-side window. He never comes back.

I'm not sure why the police officer on Route 180 lets me treat him that way. Maybe he was afraid, or maybe he was simply more professional than me. Maybe he listened to the good training officers and ignored the bad ones. As I watch him drive away, I realize I might no longer be safe to be around.

I stand on the side of the road in New Mexico and stare into the pine forests. I think, for just an instant, of walking into the wilderness of New Mexico and never coming back.

8.2

I spend a few days in Albuquerque with my aunt. In the mornings, we walk in the foothills and exercise her two Irish setters. Occasionally she violates the local ordinance and lets them off their leash. They accost a man walking by himself. When he confronts my aunt, the terrible thing in me returns. The man leaves before I can harvest it. I was going to hurt him.

My father catches a flight to Albuquerque to join me on the Southwest Chief. He loves trains, and he cannot resist the opportunity to ride the rails cross-country. I agree to have him along as a way to test my limits. If I don't hurt Dad, maybe I won't hurt Karin. We sit in the train for three days and avoid talking about Iraq. There are no accusations, no apologies, no reminiscing, and no questions. The scenery is dull and repetitive and I think how good it feels to be bored again. The train is delayed. It takes an extra day to get home. It is still too soon.

8.3

At home, I sleep with Karin. We have sex, and I feel guilty, as though I'm doing something that can't be undone. I've had little time to process what happened in Iraq. But I know that I tortured. And suddenly everything has the potential to be something I can't undo.

In the coming days, I do things that make it look as if I'm adjusting to life back home. Karin and I watch the final episode of *Friends* and go to church. During the day there is exercise, trips to the grocery, and minor league baseball games in Reading. But Iraq comes at night. There are shrinking dreams and liquid nightmares and darkroom dreams. There is a great deal of whiskey.

I run into Don Hackett at a wedding in State College. The groom was a member of First Presbyterian in Bethlehem during my high school days. Don is conducting the ceremony. We stay in a local hotel along with the rest of the wedding party. Don and his family are a few rooms down, but I don't knock on his door. I do all I can to avoid him, but we're assigned the same table at the reception, where we laugh and tell funny stories about the groom.

Don's wife is the only one to ask about Iraq. She says they were saddened to see the prison photos coming out of Abu Ghraib. She says, "I hope it wasn't like that for you." I talk a little about Abu Ghraib. Maybe I say something like "It's hard to imagine" or "It's not what you think." This is enough to silence the table. When it's awkward someone tells a story about having played ultimate Frisbee with me on the front lawn of First Presbyterian Church. He makes a joke about playing Frisbee with an interrogator from Abu Ghraib. He says, "We always thought Eric was a nice guy; now we all know better."

Karin and I take a trip with my parents to the house on Cape Cod where I spent my summers as a boy. It is August. The summer crowds are thinning out as families return their kids to school. I record a journal entry that is just an itinerary of restaurants and beaches. There are walks on Nauset Beach with Karin, and long swims in Crystal Lake in Orleans. There are fried clams and ice cream. I write about a sunset on Skaket Beach and the coffee at the Hot Chocolate Sparrow, and about a trip to Snow's, where my father and I shop for deck stain and a new downspout. The last sentence in the journal entry has something to do with wanting to move here and never go back.

8.4

We return to Bethlehem in late August. Karin goes to work and I stay at home. I take a walk on Bethlehem's south side and pass by the decaying industry. Bethlehem Steel is bankrupt now, although there are rumors about a museum and a commerce center. Some say the Smithsonian Institution will be involved. Others talk about a casino. For now, however, the buildings continue to fall apart. Bethlehem Steel has been sold to the International Steel Group. ISG decides not to revitalize the Bethlehem plant. The crumbling walls and collapsed rooftops expose the empty space inside.

At First Presbyterian Church, there is an argument about the placement of the American flag in the sanctuary. Dave Martin, the clerk of session, insists it belongs on one side, while a group of older veterans insists it belongs on the other. One of the older veterans is an usher on Sunday morning. He hands me a bulletin and escorts me down the aisle to my pew. He hands me a list of rules and regulations he copied and pasted from the Internet. One section is highlighted.

> The flag of the United States of America should hold the position
> of superior prominence, in advance of the audience, and in the posi-
> tion of honor at the clergyman's or speaker's right as he faces the
> audience.

He encourages me to talk to Dave Martin and state the case. He says no one wants to hear from the older guys. It's time for the younger generation of veterans to take their place. Everyone supports us. Everyone loves what we're doing over there.

Dave Martin has been at the church for decades. He was an engineer with Bethlehem Steel and plays saxophone in the church's contemporary worship band. Dave Martin yelled at me once after I tore up the church's front lawn playing Frisbee with a group of high school students. I approach him after the service and make the case for moving the flag to the other side of the sanctuary. He says, "You guys just don't give up. When are you going to let this go?" I spend the next month embroiled in a battle to move the flag from one side of the sanctuary to the other. There are emails and phone calls and roundtable meetings.

I visit my grandmother in the Presbyterian retirement home.

American flags and yellow ribbons now dominate the hallways. My grandmother and I talk politics. She is glad to have me home. I tell her I might go back. She hands me the pile of newspaper articles denouncing the war in Iraq. The pile has grown since I left. I concede the point. The war in Iraq is wrong. But I'm still obligated to do my part. There is still time to fix it. There is still an opportunity to do it the right way. I tell her these things as if I'm talking about U.S. policy, as if the Army can change its overall strategy and fix the problem, but I do not talk about what I've done, and I do not tell her that I'm going back in hopes of saving myself. She says, "Well, I just don't understand."

I show her pictures from Baghdad, the ones where I'm standing in front of statues or murals or landmarks. She says these are nice. We talk about the heat and the sand.

8.5

I exchange emails with Blee and Bagdasarov and learn that Blee has taken a job as an analyst at Guantánamo Bay. He says it's nothing like Iraq. Bagdasarov has accepted a job with another contracting company that is sending interrogators to Iraq. He'll conduct interrogations, but not for the Army. He'd rather do something else, but the pay is too good to turn down. He offers to put me in touch with his hiring manager, but I decline.

In September, I reapply to the NSA. I tell Karin I need a job, I need something to do, I can't just sit around and think about Iraq. And I tell the same old lie about seminary, that I'll keep it in mind and revisit the application process when the time is right. But for now, the NSA will keep me employed and keep me involved. I have every intention of using the NSA to get me back to Iraq, but I don't tell Karin this. As always, Karin doesn't want to argue. She doesn't want to tell me what I shouldn't do.

I went to Iraq the first time to reclaim my identity. I want to go back to Iraq to escape the new person I've become. I can't erase the interrogation booths, but I'm determined to replace them with something better.

Ferdinand gets a head start on his journey back to Iraq. He's in Arizona, training with DynCorp and meeting his new team members. DynCorp is taking good care of him. He has all the equipment he needs. There are weapons and body armor. He'll be serving on a protective detail for the State Department. There's still an opening for me. I tell him I'm going to give the NSA another shot. He deploys to Iraq a week later.

8.6

Though the NSA expedites my hiring, I'm still required to undergo a polygraph examination and personality test. The polygraph for the NSA is considered one of the most thorough within the intelligence community. It probes the candidate's private life in order to discover issues concerning which someone might be susceptible to blackmail or coercion. This is what the examiner says to me before beginning the test. Then he says, "Is there anything you want to tell me now?"

I sit in a room and answer questions about my driving record, criminal past, sexual behavior, and drug use. When I answer yes, I'm given the opportunity to explain my actions. When my transgressions are deemed reasonable, we move on to the next question. Every answer is thoroughly examined. The examiner encourages me to be completely honest. Any deception will be exposed once I'm hooked up to the machine.

I'm hooked up to the machine and the questions are repeated. Simple baseline questions are added to determine how I react to the truth. There are long pauses between each question. The room is dark and warm. I'm tired.

"Is your name Eric Fair?"

"No."

I've accidentally lied about my name. I was half asleep when the question was asked. My heart rate accelerates and my blood pressure increases. I feel my hands and my face warm up as the blood rushes through my veins. My body betrays me as it reacts to the lie. The examiner tells me to relax. After a long pause, he asks whether I'm ready to continue.

"Is your name Eric Fair?"

"Yes."

"Other than what we discussed earlier, have you ever done anything you're ashamed of?"

"No."

The last stage of the hiring process is a personality test and a meeting with a government psychologist. The psychologist looks over my test results. He has some concerns. He says, "There are signs of instability." He also says my answers show a tendency to put myself in a better light. He says, "You seem a bit insecure. Is there someone you're trying to impress?" I'm no longer hooked up to the polygraph machine. I tell him no.

In the late summer of 2004, I have experience in places like Abu Ghraib and Fallujah. I have firsthand knowledge of the Baath party, Ansar al-Islam, the Fedayeen Saddam, Sunnis, Shias, Chaldeans,

Iranians, Syrians, Jordanians, the Republican Guard, the Mahdi Army, and a host of individuals with connections to Al-Qaeda in Iraq. I am proficient in Arabic and conversant in the Iraqi dialect, I am knowledgeable about the growing crises in the Sunni Triangle, and I have served in a variety of positions within the intelligence community. The NSA hires me back into an entry-level position.

8.7

Karin resigns from her position as an engineer and moves with me into an apartment in Annapolis. She feels as though the job with the NSA is a good decision, and she wants to be supportive of what sounds like a promising career. But she isn't aware of the extent of my deterioration. She can't see the guilt and humiliation, and I'm not ready to admit that I've done things that can't be undone.

Karin takes a job at the front desk of the local YMCA. In the evenings, from the apartment in Annapolis, we take walks through the campus of the U.S. Naval Academy. We sign up for a tour and peer into a first-year student's room that has been opened up for the tour group. Neatly pressed uniforms line the closet. Neatly shined shoes are displayed near the bed. An older woman from the tour group says, "It looks like a prison cell." The tour guide leads us into the dining hall. There is a large mural of a naval battle from the War of 1812. The young tour guide tells a story about James Lawrence and how he died and how he said, "Don't give up the ship," and how the Naval Academy football team has adopted this as their battle cry on the football field and how recent graduates from the school are living out this creed on the battlefields of Afghanistan and Iraq. Some of them have been killed. Graduates from the Naval Academy who earn commissions in the Marine Corps are often the first to die in any war. The tour guide seems very proud of this.

We're led to the main quad, where students gather in formation prior to dinner. They stand in straight lines and march and shout and run. We are impressed that young people would sacrifice their college years for this type of commitment. We are all very proud of them.

At the NSA, I sit at a desk and read emails from other employees on a classified computer network. The email program allows users to classify messages at a variety of different levels. I write emails about meeting people for lunch or joining the office softball team. I hit the "unclassified" button for these emails. I copy and paste my contact information at the bottom. I'm admonished for including my office's alphanumeric identifier. This is classified. My supervisor sends me to a class on how to properly classify written material.

I also attend a class on PowerPoint. The NSA doesn't call it PowerPoint. The NSA paid someone to develop a program that permits users to produce classified slide shows. I learn to produce these slide shows. There are other classes, too. I report to classrooms at eight a.m. and sit through classified PowerPoint presentations until three p.m. Afterward I return to my assigned office with its classified name and try hard to properly classify internal emails that I send to coworkers.

When I'm not in a class of some kind, I do the work of an intelligence analyst. I read reports from a variety of sources about a variety of subjects. I've signed an agreement that says I can never say what is in these reports or who wrote them. This is exciting. I am ready to see the world unveiled, to understand what's really going on. To get, not vague reports about people running from the scene of an explosion or innocent detainees being suspected of anti-Coalition activities, but real information. It will be in the reports.

I never find any such reports. The reports I do read are familiar. They remind me of the reports I read or wrote in Abu Ghraib and Fallujah. They offer nothing. I ask my supervisor about the best place to find real intelligence reports. He says, "That's why we're so excited to have you in the office. The real intelligence comes from people like you in the field. The real intelligence comes from getting to know these people, getting to talk to them. Like the kind of thing you did. Interrogators get the real intelligence."

At the NSA, I read about the war almost every day, but I understand it less and less.

8.8

Karin and I begin to make Annapolis our home. We settle into a routine of early-evening walks and late-night dinners. We have favorite restaurants and favorite meals. I take a particular liking to crab cakes. We meet with a real estate agent and shop for houses in the suburbs of Washington.

In October 2004, we host an old friend from Bethlehem who wants to visit Annapolis in order to attend the annual boat show. Boat owners and dealers from around the world dock their private boats in Annapolis and open them to the public. We set aside an entire day to explore the boat show. On Saturday, October 16, 2004, we leave the apartment and head to the car. I forget my wallet. Karin and the friend wait on me while I go back to retrieve it. It is next to the computer. My email is still open. I hit the send/receive button.

> Hey Eric
> Sorry I have not written in a while. I hope that everything is going well for you. Unfortunately, this letter is not on a positive note. Just found out that Ferd was in the Green Zone Café when a suicide bomber blew it up. He is missing and presumed dead. I hope not and I am still praying that he wasn't there for some reason. Sorry to drop bad news on you but I thought that you would want to know. Other than that I am leaving in 2 and a half months. I can't wait either. Have fun and enjoy the home life.
> Mike Henson

It takes investigators two more days to find and identify Ferdinand Ibabao's body.

8.9

Somehow I am embarrassed by Ferdinand's death, as though it might ruin the day at the boat show. I feel ashamed when I tell Karin, and assure her and our friend that we should continue on as planned. I don't want to tell them what I'm thinking. Maybe Ferdinand deserved to die in Iraq. Maybe I deserve to die there, too.

The boat show is crowded. We start our day in the section dedicated to catamarans. You wouldn't think there's much room in a catamaran, but the designers manage to fit entire living areas in the hulls. The rooms are cramped, but everything you could want in a house is there. The same is true of other sailboats. Some of the largest even have movie theaters. But the real highlight of the show is the full-power section. These amazing boats are miniature mansions. We marvel at the luxury. Each room is engineered to maximize space. Nothing is wasted. There is storage behind every door. The beds are comfortable. Each room has a flat-screen television. I sit on the bridge of one of the largest boats and let Karin take my picture.

We eat lunch on the water. I have clam chowder, the New England kind. Our friend from Bethlehem gets crab cakes at an outdoor stand. We tell him there are much better places for crab cakes, but he seems to enjoy the ones he has. We spend another hour or two at the boat show, but when the afternoon sun drains our energy, we return to the apartment and send our friend on his way.

On Sunday, the final day of the boat show, there is a fireworks display out over the Chesapeake Bay. There is a thump, like someone slamming a door. Then more. Then the growl of rockets. They overshoot and detonate out over the water. I return to the apartment and drink too much whiskey.

8.10

The NSA has an internal publication, distributed throughout the agency, with articles by senior managers and career intelligence professionals. There is a special interest section where employees write about their careers and give advice on how best to excel in a career with the NSA. One section in particular introduces new employees. My supervisor says I've been selected to appear in this section. He tells me to write out my bio and list my experiences. This will be the first time I write about Iraq.

The editor of the publication gets back in touch with me and says he's interested in how my experience as an interrogator influences my work at the NSA. He says I should consider a full article. He says it will likely be the lead story. He says, "Short stories, vignettes. Help us to walk in your shoes. Help us to know what you were thinking." I write the editor and tell him that maybe now isn't the right time to write an article about interrogation. He encourages me to push forward.

The article is published in two parts. In the original version, I question the efficacy of certain intelligence-gathering techniques and wonder whether, for the sake of morality, it might be best to sacrifice some level of tactical knowledge. I was asked to rewrite this section. I cut it completely. Instead, I wrote about how my experience in the interrogation booths had familiarized me with the overall intelligence cycle. The article is well received. I take phone calls from a variety of managers and supervisors who are excited to work with me. Doors at the NSA begin to open.

On Sundays, Karin and I shop for a new church. A friend recommends a Presbyterian church just north of Annapolis, a Presbyterian Church of America (PCA) congregation. This is not the Presbyterian church of my ancestors. We know PCA as the Presbyterians who don't ordain women and who supported slavery. In the bulletin, Karin points out a section about the history of the PCA, specifically the part about the traditional role of women. Women are not allowed to teach adult Sunday school classes in the PCA.

Karin and I stop attending the church.

In November 2004, I submit my name for an opening in Iraq with the NSA. Most new hires are expected to spend at least two years with the agency before applying for an overseas tour, but my experience, combined with the lack of NSA employees interested in deploying to Iraq, has made me a viable candidate. My supervisor says that if no one else applies, the slot will be mine. There are no other applicants. I accept the offer and begin preparations for a return to Iraq.

Karin and I spend Thanksgiving with my parents in Bethlehem. We stay in my old room. The full-length mirror on the closet is still decorated with Boston Red Sox stickers and a photograph of Wade Boggs. From the window I can see Martin Tower, the twenty-one-story skyscraper that served as Bethlehem Steel's headquarters. When I was a boy, Martin Tower lit up the night. Smaller businesses occupy the tower now, but each year fewer and fewer remain. The tower grows darker as more lights are turned off.

I tell my parents about going back to Iraq. My mother rolls her eyes and leaves the room. My father is confrontational. He says he doesn't understand. He says, "Can you explain it to me?" I cannot. He's right. I shouldn't be going back. But just like the first time I left for Iraq, I decide not to listen to him. I don't want him to know what I've done. I want a new experience so I don't have to tell him the truth.

I ride with my father to the farmers' market in Allentown. We buy ring bologna and pierogies. We stand in line for shoofly pie. We decide the wet-bottom kind is best.

8.11

The NSA's deployment process is far more thorough than CACI's. But, like CACI, the NSA doesn't look into my health. No one asks about my heart. There is no reason to. By all appearances, I am healthy. I haven't seen a cardiologist since those last days with the Bethlehem Police Department in the summer of 2003. I don't question the diagnosis, but I remain unwilling to accept that things have changed for me. So I continue on and pretend I am healthy.

On April 1, 2005, a month before I leave for Iraq, Karin rushes into the apartment in Annapolis, sounding concerned. She has been listening to NPR. There was a report about explosions in Vermont. Apparently a downturn in the maple syrup market is having an adverse effect on maple trees. They aren't being tapped for syrup often enough. The syrup is building up inside the trees, causing them to explode.

I want to laugh, but she's quite serious. We head out for an errand. We turn on NPR and the story about the explosions in Vermont comes on again. Robert Siegel is serious and sincere. The report is wonderfully over the top and ludicrous. In the background, there is a cartoonish explosion of an untapped maple tree. Robert Siegel says there have been injuries. Some unfortunate souls have even been killed. I cover my eyes, shake my head, and try not to laugh. Another maple tree detonates. Karin is desperate to believe, but the story becomes more ridiculous. She hangs on for as long as she can before surrendering to the obvious. It is April Fool's Day.

Karin is innocent. She is honest. She thinks everyone else is the same. If NPR tells her that maple trees are exploding, she believes it. I tell her I am going back to Iraq for the right reasons. She believes that, too.

In May 2005, Karin drives me to BWI. As we approach the airport, I think about how long it will take to get to the passenger terminal in Kuwait. That was the last place I saw Ferdinand. My stomach burns and cramps. I tell Karin to pull into a 7-Eleven. My bowels explode as I sit on the filthy toilet in the back.

9

Back in Baghdad, I sleep better than I did in Annapolis. I live in a small, opulent building in a secluded corner of Camp Slayer, an American base adjacent to Camp Victory where an array of units with secretive-sounding names have set up shop. Our buildings, which likely housed the most privileged members of the Baath party, are made of marble and stone, adorned with columns and archways. We don't call ourselves the NSA. We call ourselves the Cryptological Support Group (CSG). It's no secret that secret units call themselves support groups. We live next to the Tactical Deployment Support Group, the Combat Logistics Support Group, and the Naval Warfare Support Group.

For a few weeks, I do well, and I'm tempted to think that I just might be able to return from this deployment feeling different. I'm well rested, well fed, and sober. In the mornings, I run the perimeter of Camp Slayer. The camp occupies the grounds of the old Baath party headquarters where a man-made lake serves as the centerpiece for a series of palaces and mansions with boat launches and swimming pools. Most of these have been partially destroyed by Coalition bombs. Some have been reduced to rubble. Chain-link fences have been erected to keep personnel from exploring the ruins, but the fence lines are incomplete, as if someone abandoned the project halfway through after deciding it wasn't worth the effort.

Near one palace is a synthetic mountain made of cement and rebar and designed as a play area for Baath party children, a sort of Disneyland for the kids whose parents knew the right people. The mountain is a labyrinth of tunnels and jungle gyms and hiding places. I make my way to the top of the mountain, where a sitting area provides panoramic views of the entire complex. There are statues of animals for children to climb on. Most of the statues are missing their heads.

I work on Camp Victory. Camp Victory and Camp Slayer are part of the same base complex, so there is no need to travel out into any unsecured portion of Iraq. I am protected by blast walls and guard towers. We make the five-minute drive in heavily armored vehicles. A Marine Corps gunnery sergeant serves as our driver. He says the vehicles don't meet ██ standards. ████████████ ████████████ These are armored only to level III. Level IV vehicles will arrive next week. For now, we settle for armor that can stop small-arms fire and RPGs, but won't survive a direct strike by an IED. There are no IEDs on Camp Victory.

Before driving to work, we inventory body armor and weapons that are stored in a secure room on Camp Slayer. The body armor is the most advanced style issued to troops in Iraq. I am assigned an assault rifle and a handgun. There are cases of modern holsters and slings and boxes of ammunition. We leave all of it behind. We never leave Camp Victory.

In the summer of 2005, there is less talk than there had been a year ago about the war in Iraq coming to an end. The pace of mortar and rocket attacks has slowed, but only because insurgents have begun to discover the true advantage of IEDs. Iraq's roads are more dangerous than ever, and the route between Camp Victory and the Green Zone in downtown Baghdad has become especially perilous. The Army calls the road Route Irish. Soldiers call it Route Ambush.

As it is for so many organizations in Iraq, protecting against IEDs has become a focus of the NSA. During the day, I read reports about the IEDs that detonate just beyond the walls where I spend my days drinking Gatorade and eating Doritos. I read about how far a vehicle's axle was thrown from the explosion, about debris that lands a few blocks away. I read about the types of injuries that IEDs inflict, and about impact craters, blast radiuses, daisy chains, and artillery rounds. Then I look at the photos. I'm supposed to be looking for indicators that will allow analysts and technicians to begin to take preventative measures, but I'm drawn to the severed limbs and pools of blood. I think the blood should soak into the dirt of Iraq, but it doesn't. It settles in bright red pools, like spilled paint.

I spend a great deal of effort learning about a type of IED called an explosively formed projectile (EFP). The EFP is an ingenious invention that uses explosives to shape a piece of metal in such a way that it can penetrate armor. EFPs are effective in eliminating the driver of a vehicle. The photographs are particularly gruesome. The target vehicle isn't shredded and burned, the way it is in standard IED attacks. Instead, the projectile minces whatever is inside. I read a great deal about EFP attacks, but I eventually stop looking at pictures.

My days are long. Sometimes, I take an hour for lunch and tend to administrative details around Camp Victory. I update my ID badge or attend briefings with other civilians who work for other support groups. After the briefings, I go to the PX and buy more Gatorade and Doritos. I stand in line at the chow hall and stare at the other civilians, wondering if any of them work for CACI. I avoid the soldiers who reek of dirt and sweat, their uniforms stained with oblong salt circles from hour-long convoys on Route Irish. I think of their limbs appearing in the photos that I look at as I work. I sit at a table decorated with red, white, and blue bunting and watch ESPN on a flat-screen TV. Ferdinand and I sat at this table during one of his visits from Fallujah. It's here that we talked about interrogation and the Palestinian chair. Tyner was using it more and more. Jim Fisk was conducting interrogations again. I think of the explosion that killed Ferdinand. I think about where his limbs ended up.

At work I have access to an enormous database of reports and photographs of attacks that have taken place throughout Iraq. The attack that killed Ferdinand is easy to find; it is one of the few cases of a suicide bomber infiltrating the myriad security checkpoints of the Green Zone. I read the reports. I look at the pictures.

9.1

I spend most of my days in front of a computer screen, sending emails and exchanging information in a variety of chat rooms with other intelligence agencies and services. I am the NSA's subject matter expert on intelligence concerns in Iraq. Dozens of analysts, linguists, and intelligence professionals from around the world rely on me to act as a liaison to a variety of civilian and military organizations in Iraq. This is the sort of thing I'll write on my internal résumé. But, like most analysts in Iraq, I spend much of my day playing solitaire and Minesweeper.

In the lower left-hand corner of my computer screen is an icon labeled "Pie Chart of Death." I don't know whether it's an approved NSA program or just a laugh some analyst snuck onto the computer. I enter my dates of service into the Pie Chart of Death. The program generates a pink-and-blue pie chart depicting how much time I have left in my three-month tour. The pink portion of the pie chart shows how much time I've served. The blue portion shows how much time I have remaining. If you expand the window to take up the entire screen, you can actually see the line on the pie chart move from day to day.

Heavily armed U.S. soldiers secure the compound where I work. They pretend not to know who works on the compound. They search us when we enter and they search us when we leave. Reinforced walls and concertina wire surround the buildings. ████████████ ██ ██ There is a small trailer used by a support group with employees who live in places like Arlington, McLean, and Langley, Virginia. I enter this trailer from time to time to share information with this support group. I also show them how to access the Pie Chart of Death.

During the week, civilian contractors from various countries around the world enter the compound to clean the toilets and vacuum the floors. The Army calls them third country nationals (TCNs). The TCNs who clean our compound are from Egypt. As I sit at my computer and update the Pie Chart of Death, a group of TCNs enter the room without warning. This is a major security breach. Classified maps, photographs, and PowerPoint presentations adorn the walls. We are supposed to receive warning before TCNs enter the room. The TCNs have come to change the lightbulbs. The Army insists that the lightbulbs be changed every week. They assign TCNs from Egypt to do this work inside our highly classified compound.

I track down the Army sergeant responsible for maintaining the facility and scheduling maintenance. I tell her that I'd be happy to change the lightbulbs myself. This would prevent further problems with security and TCNs. This makes her angry. She insists that she alone is responsible for making decisions that pertain to the maintenance of the compound. I say something like "Look, be serious" or "Hey, c'mon." She erupts. I try to calm her down. I say, "I'm like you, I used to be a soldier." She says, "You're a fucking soldier? What's your fucking rank, soldier?" I say that I'm not a soldier. I'm just an analyst with the NSA. I say the security breach is a big deal and I don't want it to get her into trouble. This makes her angrier. I say, "Look, imagine if we allowed East German nationals to come into the NSA and change the lightbulbs during the Cold War?" Now she's losing it, so I say more things. Every employee of every secretive support group has come out of their trailer to see the angry sergeant get angrier and angrier. From a distance, she must look furious and aggressive. Up close, I see she is about to cry.

Eventually I get the lightbulbs. A few weeks later, there is another security breach when a detail of TCNs arrives to clean our keyboards and monitors. I don't approach the sergeant this time. Instead, I show the TCNs the Pie Chart of Death. I practice speaking Arabic with them.

9.2

The Army has its own secret intelligence unit in Iraq. They don't call it a support group. They call it the Analysis and Control Element (ACE). It's made up of young enlisted soldiers with high-level security clearances who know how to properly classify PowerPoint presentations and emails. I discover that one of the young soldiers from the ACE is responsible for writing the Pie Chart of Death program and loading it onto our computers in the CSG.

The ACE requests information on EFPs and I'm sent to brief them. When I arrive, I'm directed to the officer in charge of the ACE. Like all officers in charge of a unit like the ACE, he is a career military man, a professional employee of the U.S. Army who will likely spend his working life in uniform. Directing an intelligence unit like the ACE is considered a critical step in a professional officer's development. Directing that same office in a combat zone is an invaluable bullet point on an officer's résumé. The position is reserved for the best officers, some of whom will be generals someday. The officer in charge of the ACE in Iraq is a lieutenant colonel. He has over fifteen years in uniform. He went to Dartmouth. He has a graduate degree and a commanding presence. He gives me an impressive officer speech.

The officer tells me he works alongside a civilian counterpart. This person will be my contact at the ACE. He assures me his counterpart is his equal and I should afford him the same level of respect. The counterpart, he tells me, has similar credentials and experience. He has held similar positions in the military. The counterpart is a civilian contractor. He works for CACI. The officer introduces me to Jim Fisk.

When Jim and I go to lunch that day, I tell him he's a liar. He says I should know how this works by now. He says he's just doing what CACI tells him to do. He says he took the job at the ACE because CACI offered it to him. Besides, who else was going to take it?

We sit down for lunch at the same table in the dining hall where Ferdinand and I talked about the Palestinian chair. Jim doesn't want to talk about Fallujah. He spent a few more months there before being called back to Baghdad. By late 2004, more and more CACI employees had quit. Those of us who were hired in 2003 and remained became the most senior employees. As CACI struggled to find suitable candidates for a variety of positions, the company promoted from within. Jim started working at the ACE under the supervision of another CACI employee. When that employee quit, Jim became the civilian counterpart of an Army lieutenant colonel. Jim does not have a college degree. He has less than four years in the Army. But I answer to him.

In the coming weeks, I avoid the ACE. I assign other employees to give the briefings or I send classified PowerPoint presentations through classified email. I warn other NSA employees to stay away from Jim Fisk. They don't. They attend a briefing with him. Jim gives a classified briefing to an Army general. Halfway through, the general stops the briefing and berates the entire team for incompetence. The NSA employees return to the CSG. They say, "You were right." Jim remains at the ACE, but I never hear from him again.

9.3

For the first six weeks of my second deployment, I enjoy Iraq, my morning runs and my hot showers and my quiet air-conditioned rides in armored vehicles to Camp Victory. I enjoy my ham-and-cheese omelets. The cook with gray hair makes the best ones. He adds just the right amount of ham. I enjoy ESPN, haircuts, Gatorade, and Doritos. I enjoy working sixteen-hour days. I log the extra hours on my pay chart, adding up the overtime pay I'll collect when I get home. I enjoy returning to the CSG at night and playing Ping-Pong on a sheet of plywood. Soldiers draw dirty pictures in the dust from the sandstorms. I enjoy sitting outside, smoking a cigar, and watching the helicopters fly overhead. I enjoy the packages I get from Karin.

In late May, as the heat of the Iraqi summer begins to burn, Karin sends me a package for my birthday. As a joke, she includes a package of edible gummy soldiers. The package bakes in the heat of the afternoon. The gummy soldiers melt and bond together. I send Karin an email and make a joke about the gummy soldiers becoming a cohesive unit. This is the joke I'll tell people when they ask about Iraq. I won't talk about Abu Ghraib, or Fallujah, or Walid and Thaer. I'll talk about the gummy soldiers melting. People like this story.

A sandstorm blows through Baghdad and covers everything in a fine dust. Most of us have allergic reactions and spend the next week nursing sore throats and painful coughs. Some become especially ill. I'm familiar with Camp Victory, so I volunteer to drive the sickest employees to the medical clinic. The clinic is near the morgue where I unzipped the body bag and tried to identify Walid or Thaer's body. I park under a tree while the others seek attention inside the clinic. I listen to music on the radio. I read a Ken Follett novel. I recline the seat and try to nap, but nothing I do can distract me from the memory of the morgue. I see Walid. My mind opens the bag and forces me to see the images again. Closing my eyes makes it worse. I remember lifting the bag and feeling the boy fall apart.

That night I send an email to Karin and ask her to smuggle alcohol inside the next care package. I don't write anything about Ping-Pong or ham-and-cheese omelets or morning runs around the man-made lakes. Instead, I give specific instructions about buying the miniature bottles of vodka and whiskey you get at the front counter at the liquor store. I tell her to conceal them inside cartons of Fig Newtons and Ritz crackers. Karin does this. Within a week, I have whiskey again. After the trip to the morgue, the nightmares are back. The alcohol helps.

9.4

At the CSG, I work with another analyst who is about my age. Like me, he volunteered for Iraq when no one else from his office was willing to go. He has a technical degree from Brigham Young University. We talk about Mormons and Christians; we agree that neither of our churches is doing enough to clarify its position on war.

The lieutenant colonel in charge of the CSG calls a meeting: an Army unit needs intelligence support. He's looking for volunteers to give a briefing. The briefing will take place at Abu Ghraib.

The analyst from BYU is the first to volunteer. The colonel thanks him. After the meeting, I talk to the analyst about Abu Ghraib. I tell him to reconsider. I tell him not to go. He says he came to Iraq to do his part. He's bored at the CSG. He's tired of spending his days in front of a computer screen. He wants to see the real thing. The lieutenant colonel asks me to accompany the analyst from BYU. He says it will be helpful to have someone along who knows the lay of the land.

At the last minute, the briefing location is changed to Camp Victory. The analyst is disappointed. The lieutenant colonel calls him a "hard charger." He says, "We need more guys like you willing to get out there." He says, "Don't worry, you'll get your chance."

9.5

In the morning, I'm assigned one of the armored vehicles and sent on my way. The trip to the ███████████ facility takes me past the morgue. It takes me past CACIville. It takes me past the terminal where Ferdinand and I flew out of Iraq.

At the ███████████ facility I feel sick. I use the blue portable toilet outside the gate. I sit inside and struggle to breathe. Don Hackett would say that God meets you wherever you are. I want God to wait outside.

The officer in charge of the facility introduces a group of civilians and thanks them for their willingness to contribute to the effort. He refers to them as professional subject matter experts. He says, "We're lucky to have these guys on board." Then he introduces a group of CACI contractors led by Randy Kutcher.

I haven't seen Randy since I left him at Abu Ghraib. At the time, he was earning a reputation as a solid analyst despite the fact that he had no experience in the field. Now, he serves as the lead analyst

for detainee issues on Camp Victory. Randy is competent, but like Jim Fisk, he appears unqualified to hold his position.

As I continue to work with a variety of intelligence units in Iraq, I come across more and more CACI employees in powerful positions. Some are qualified; most are not. But because the war in Iraq is still in its initial phase, CACI employees have spent more time in Iraq than many of their military counterparts. Without rank on their collars or badges on their chests, there is no way to determine their professional experience or competence. The Army is quick to defer to them.

9.6

The ▮▮▮▮▮▮▮ facility at Camp Victory was recently renovated. The concrete buildings are clean and sterile. ▮▮▮▮▮▮▮ The doors have windows. The hallways are well lit. ▮▮▮▮▮ and ▮▮▮▮ The supervising officer welcomes me inside the facility.

He asks for advice.

The ▮▮▮▮▮ booth is neat and well organized. The room is outfitted with adjustable office chairs, the kind you buy at Office Depot. There is a large wooden table, too heavy to throw. There is a carpet on the floor. There are no marks on the walls. ▮▮▮ is led into the room by two military policemen. They remove his handcuffs and place them on the table. ▮▮▮▮

The NSA collects, processes, and disseminates intelligence information from foreign signals for intelligence and counterintelligence purposes and to support military operations. This is what the NSA website says. What it means is that, while imperfect, the NSA is capable of providing accurate information on foreigners and their activities. Unlike the CIA, the NSA doesn't draw conclusions or make assumptions. Signals intelligence is unambiguous. █████████

████████████████ There is no doubt about his guilt. He wasn't seen running from the scene of an explosion. He isn't just suspected of anti-Coalition activities. His jealous neighbor didn't turn him in because of an old grudge. It doesn't matter if he's Sunni or Shia. He has done terrible things to his fellow countrymen, and he has done terrible things to U.S. soldiers. There is hard evidence to prove this. This will not be an ███████████████ about determining guilt. This will be about gathering critical information from a man who wields great power and has done terrible things on the streets of Iraq.

9.7

I return to Minesweeper and the Pie Chart of Death. The pink section is beginning to overtake the blue. I read emails from other NSA employees and play Ping-Pong on the sheet of plywood. That night, I drink the rest of the alcohol Karin concealed in the box of Fig Newtons. I send her a message asking for more. I tell her to forget the miniature bottles. Buy a bottle of mouthwash. Pour it out. Replace it with liquor. Send two.

The next day I'm pulled aside by the CSG supervisor. ██ I get sick in the portable toilet and tell God to wait outside. ███

There is to be no redemption for me in Iraq.

9.8

I no longer sleep well. I no longer enjoy myself. A package from Karin arrives. It has the two mouthwash bottles filled with liquor. I send an email and ask for more.

I am not disgusted by my actions.

I am disgusted by how good it felt to wield power
I am terrified of where else that feeling might take me. In Iraq, I have

not just taken the wrong path. I have walked in the wrong direction entirely.

9.9

My replacement arrives at the Baghdad airport. I drive one of the new armored vehicles to pick her up. The vehicle is an enormous Ford F-250 pickup truck. The armor is thick enough to stop the most advanced IEDs. The windows are so thick as to distort the view of the road. The headlights and taillights are encased in steel cages. The truck is equipped with an enormous engine and a custom suspension system in order to bear the crushing weight of all the armor. It is the safest vehicle I have ever driven, yet it will never leave Camp Victory.

The replacement is eager to get to work. █████████ ███████████████████████████ She says she heard I was at Abu Ghraib. She says, "That's impressive." ███████████████████████████████

At the office, I show her Minesweeper and the Pie Chart of Death. The pink section of my pie chart is just about complete. I have less than a week remaining. I show her the Ping-Pong table and where to get the best ham-and-cheese omelets. I tell her how to smuggle alcohol into the country. She says, "I don't think we're supposed to be doing that."

At the last minute, another opportunity in Iraq becomes available. Another unit is looking for support. I have the necessary qualifications. It will extend my deployment an additional two months. ████████████████████████████████ I volunteer, but my supervisor tells me it's time to go home, but I don't know how.

9.10

In July 2005, for the first time since Abu Ghraib, I attend a chapel service in Iraq. It's the same chapel I ignored after the day with Walid and his body. There is still a large television where soldiers shoot each other on the screen. Paris Hilton is still on the magazine rack; her cover photo shows wear and tear from too many trips to the portable toilets. Inside the chapel, there are aluminum folding chairs and an altar made of plywood. A loaf of bread and Hi-C grape drink will be served for Communion.

During the sermon, the chaplain references a well-known poem about footprints in the sand. The poem's narrator describes two sets of footprints, one for God, one for the believer. Occasionally, one set of footprints disappears. This is when God carries us.

I think of the portable toilets outside the ███████████ facility at Camp Victory. I think of all the sets of footprints I left while walking into ███████████ facilities. I think of God living in the prison with the detainees. The footprints that lead inside are mine.

I leave Iraq in August 2005. Karin meets me at BWI. We walk back to the car together. She's lost weight. I have, too. After three months in Iraq, I sleep with her and pretend I'm home.

10

Back at Fort Meade, I have thirty minutes for lunch. I take forty-five. No one cares. I take the long way back. From the cafeteria I walk into the main rotunda across the shiny floor engraved with the NSA seal. I take the escalators to the third floor. They're slower than the elevators. At the top of the second escalator, I feel sweat on my forehead. I lean to one side. The room leans with me, then spins, then darkens. There is an open lobby at the top of the escalator, then a short walk to a long overpass that leads to my building. I won't make it that far. The escalators and hallways are filled with other NSA employees returning to their offices from long lunches, so I'm forced to move out of the way. I ease myself onto the floor, but no one stops to help. At the NSA there is a joke about introverts and extroverts. Introverts, they say, walk the halls and stare at their own shoes. Extroverts, they say, stare at other people's shoes. No one stares at me. They just walk by. This is my heart failing.

A nurse at the NSA calls it a vasovagal response, a simple fainting spell. It isn't. It's heart failure. I've ignored my heart condition for more than five years. My heart has deteriorated. It is weaker. It is desperate for blood, so it steals blood from the brain. This is the beginning of my end.

At the cardiologist's office, I read the pamphlets with pictures of old people. There are articles about low-salt diets and proper exercise routines. There are advertisements for beta blockers and ACE inhibitors. There are statistics about successful procedures and surgeries. The cardiologist says no more trips to Iraq. He's concerned about the escalator incident. He talks about warning signs. He talks about cardiac arrest. He talks about sudden death. He says, "Who in hell let you go to Iraq?"

My father never took a sick day. In thirty-five years of teaching, he never missed a day of work. "It's just the right way to do things," he would say. At the NSA, after my deployment, I take sick days as often as I can. I lie to my supervisor about sore throats and low-grade fevers. I tell Karin it doesn't make me feel guilty. She leaves for work and I go back to bed. I drink whiskey at lunch, then pour out the rest of the bottle. I drive to the liquor store and buy a new one. I drink enough of the new bottle to match yesterday's level so that Karin won't notice the difference. At night, I drink from that bottle, too. Sometimes I drink the whole thing. This complicates the next day. I buy a new bottle and hope Karin forgets where it all started.

She does not forget. Karin pays the bills, does the taxes, and keeps the records. She keeps the apartment organized. She cleans and organizes everything in the house, from the dirty dishes to the empty bottles. This is her way of showing love. But I hate it. I do not want someone to bring order to my life. I do not want to be told that I'm making poor decisions and drinking too much. Karin's order exposes me. I hate her for it.

My cardiologists recommend that I refrain from physical exercise, but I ignore them. I'm starting to feel sick now, but I still refuse to accept that anything has changed. So after work, I go on runs through Annapolis. The heat and humidity of Maryland make it difficult to breathe at times. I feel weak.

In October, Karin and I sign up for the Army Ten-Miler. She passes me at mile five. Young kids start passing me at mile six. At mile seven, just past the Lincoln Memorial, the race is rerouted.

There's been a bomb scare at the finish line. We're forced to run an additional mile to an alternate finishing area. There's no water or food. After that, I walk another mile to the Metro. My chest heaves as my heart and lungs struggle to process the air. There is another fainting incident. Other runners stop to help. It takes me longer to get up. The cardiologist says, "Are you trying to die?"

Death scares me. Or at least, an easy one does. I do not want to die on an escalator or in an air-conditioned hallway or at the end of the Army Ten-Miler. I wanted to die in Iraq. I wanted to die like Ferdinand. That would have been fair. I wouldn't owe anything. Instead, I have a debt to pay. For Abu Ghraib and Fallujah. For the Palestinian chair.

At the NSA, I attend an awards ceremony for employees who have deployed to hazardous-duty stations throughout the world. Those who went to Iraq and Afghanistan are given special attention. High-ranking officers and civilians stand up front and talk about the ways the NSA is changing. There is a general consensus that the agency must become more aggressive and less risk averse in pursuing targets. The agency will need employees like us, willing to take the fight to the enemy. A new chapter is opening for the NSA, one that will launch us on missions never before considered. The speaker attempts to impersonate Jack Nicholson in the movie *A Few Good Men*. He says, "The American public needs us in the shadows, they want us in the shadows, and they will sleep better at night because we are in the shadows." The audience laughs. Then he says, "It's a new world. It's a new NSA."

An Army colonel takes the podium and gives a speech about why men go to war. It is the speech about a grandfather and his grandchildren. I heard the speech at basic training, at Fort Benning, and at language school. I heard it almost every other week with the 101st Airborne. I even heard a version of it at the police academy. A grandfather is talking to his grandchildren. In some versions, they are sitting on his lap; in other versions, they are standing at his bedside. The grandchildren ask the grandfather questions about his life. They ask him about whatever war defined his generation. Sometimes it's

World War I, or Vietnam, or Korea. Mostly it's World War II. The grandchildren want to know what the grandfather did during the war. Then the story ends. The audience is left to consider the shame of a grandfather who can't say he did his part. Sometimes the speech includes a quote about people sleeping well at night because of rough men willing to do violence on their behalf. Sometimes it is George Orwell saying this, or Teddy Roosevelt, or Rudyard Kipling. Mostly it's Winston Churchill.

I play a round of golf with an old friend from the 101st. Like me, he served on an LLVI team. He was recruited by the same secretive unit that once recruited me. Unlike me, he stayed in and took the position. He's stationed at Fort Meade now. He travels to Iraq and Afghanistan often. He's seen terrible things. He's done terrible things. We talk about buying new drivers and pitching wedges. We talk about whether it's better to be in a sand trap or in the rough. We play dollar skins. He wins most of the holes, then refuses to collect the money. On the eighteenth fairway, we dare each other to hit into the foursome that refused to let us play through. Afterward, we drink beer and eat turkey club sandwiches. The Baltimore Ravens are on TV.

On the weekend, Karin and I return to Bethlehem and visit old friends. At dinner, one of these old friends asks what I think about Iraq. He asks this after he's told me what he thinks about Iraq. Another friend talks about her father who served in Vietnam. He never talked about what he did, and they always respected him for this. He didn't need to brag about his war. He was a silent warrior.

After dinner, we return to the friend's apartment. Her elderly neighbors need help moving an air-conditioning unit out of the attic. She introduces the old man as a World War II vet. She says, "You two can talk." The old man is embarrassed about needing help with the air-conditioning unit. When we're alone, he says something about Iraq. He says he could tell we had it bad over there. I ask about Europe. He was a crewmember on a B-17. He says, "Of course I don't talk about it. I killed a lot of people." He talks about the initial excitement of dropping bombs. Then he talks about finding out where the bombs were landing. He talks about finding out about the people the bombs were landing on. He talks about the families that were down below. The children. He says, "I don't think that gets forgiven."

When we're done moving the air-conditioning unit, we go back to my friend's apartment. She thanks me for my help. She says, "Thanks for talking to Frank. He never talks about the war. I'm sure it was good for him."

Frank dies a few months later. My heart will kill me long before I have grandchildren who can ask me what I did during the war. In the meantime, I keep drinking.

10.1

It is September 2005. I've been back from Iraq for two months. It's clear now that the insurgency is not in its last throes. There is more war to see, but I no longer have the courage or desire to see it. My career at the NSA is beginning to take shape. I've nearly completed my training program and will likely be promoted by the end of the year. My salary is rising. All I want to do is quit.

At night, I scream. The nightmares are all but intolerable now. Alcohol no longer has the effect I've relied on since those first inter-rogations at Abu Ghraib. It's been nearly two years. Things will get worse.

We sit through a sermon at an independent church in Annapolis that has a projector and a pull-down screen. In the middle of the sermon, the pastor stops to play a clip from a movie. It's *Napoleon Dynamite*. Two brothers are arguing. One stands up and slaps the other across the face. The congregation laughs and the pastor makes a point.

The sermon is terrible. The music is terrible. The children's chat is terrible. For the first time, I leave a church service before it's over.

That same month I reapply to the Princeton Theological Semi-nary. I tell myself I can't do worse than the *Napoleon Dynamite* sermon. But the truth is that seminary is my final hope for redemption. I should have listened when friends and family told me not to go to Iraq. They told me they always thought of me as a Presbyterian pastor. But those voices are no longer telling me to go to seminary. By the time I get there, I'll come to find that it is too late.

10.2

The application packet is similar to the one from 2003. It asks questions about my call to ministry. I do not write about my heart this time. I write about Iraq. I write about God's role in war. I write about not knowing whether God orchestrates pain or abandons us to it, and how God is either powerless to confront evil, or complicit in its presence. I desire to stand before God and ask him questions about all the terrible things that have happened. God has an obligation to answer these questions. I'm drunk when I write these things. I'm drunk or hungover every day now. By the time I'm sober, or at least less drunk, I've already driven to the post office and mailed the packet. I expect to be rejected again.

Two weeks later, I travel to the seminary for a campus tour and an interview. There is a large group meeting about financial aid, at which students ask questions about the application process. A number of students who have traveled long distances failed to schedule interviews. Local applicants are asked to surrender their time slots and reschedule for a later date. I ask whether this will affect our application timeline. A representative from the admissions office asks for my name and retrieves my packet. He says, "You're the Iraq guy. Don't worry, you're already accepted."

10.3

Karin's parents come to visit; they bring a bottle of wine, along with an expensive Norwegian liquor. They say it's the kind of thing we can serve for special occasions. I consume the entire bottle in two nights, and then try to hide it by burying it in the bottom of the recycling bin.

Karin cleans and organizes the bottles and cans in the recycling bin before putting them to the curb. I return to the apartment and find the kitchen counter lined with the bottles and cans she has meticulously scrubbed and set out to dry. I find the bottle of liquor from Norway. I'm embarrassed, so I lash out. For the first time, we argue about alcohol. This is also the first time I remember her trying to stand her ground and tell me something is wrong. She says something about the alcohol getting worse. I say something about how I don't deserve to have things taken away from me. As the argument drags on, I'm surprised by how long she stands her ground. She even has the courage to wonder aloud if they allow alcohol at seminary. I tell her to go to hell.

10.4

In November 2005, when we're talking again, Karin and I decide it's time to leave Maryland and go home to Bethlehem. Karin has received an offer to return to the chemical company in Allentown as a process engineer. Iraq continues to deteriorate. It will be a long war. If I stay with the NSA, there will be more trips overseas. I am tempted. I could spend significant time in Iraq and make significant money. I could eventually take another job as a contractor and work as an intelligence analyst full-time in Iraq. I wouldn't have to see Karin. There would be no living expenses. I could do it for five or six years. I'd be wealthy. I could divorce Karin and move somewhere on my own to die of heart failure.

I've been changing jobs and relocating ever since the heart diagnosis. The decision to apply to Princeton is foolish, but I'm too unstable to see that. Karin is, too. Her wounds are as deep as mine. The war has damaged her as much as it has me, and we struggle to find a solution; we struggle to find a way back to where we were. I search for something to define me, so I'll become a pastor. Karin searches for parity. She hasn't suffered enough. She hasn't lost anything. She hasn't been to war, so she surrenders to whatever I say. We're both trying to make things even again. We're both making things so much worse.

At the NSA, I meet with my supervisor. She says, "We'd have lost you to the CIA eventually." She talks about a new program at the NSA. They're looking for people willing to spend significant time in Iraq. She says someone with my credentials would be perfect for the position. She says, "You were born for this war. Why not give it another year?"

The office organizes a going-away party. The supervisor stands up front and compares me to Jack Bauer of *24*. She says, "God help the terrorist who comes to your church." Then they present me with gifts. There is a nice aerial photo of the camp where I worked in Iraq. It is classified, so I have to leave it behind. There is a certificate of appreciation from a supporting office, and a shopping bag filled with cheap gifts from the official NSA store. There is a lanyard, a plastic coffee mug, a key chain, and a glass sculpture engraved with the NSA seal. I hold up the sculpture and say, "I'll be sure to display this from the pulpit so everyone knows you're listening."

10.5

In Bethlehem, we buy a house on Bonus Hill. There are wood floors, plaster walls, high ceilings, and cast-iron radiators. We remodel the ninety-year-old fireplace and install a wood-burning stove. We go to a quarry and pick out the stone that will line the new chimney. I sit in front of the fire and start reading books again. Someone recommends *One Bullet Away* by Nathaniel Fick. Fick recounts his time as a platoon leader in the Marine Corps with deployments to Afghanistan and Iraq. It is a heroic story. Someone else recommends *The Irresistible Revolution,* by Shane Claiborne. Claiborne studied at Princeton Theological Seminary before dropping out to serve the poor in Philadelphia. He traveled to Iraq in 2003 and served as a human shield during the run-up to the invasion. This feels heroic, too. I wish my story was like one of these.

To our surprise, life improves. In January 2006, Karin and I spend a weekend in the Pocono Mountains. We laugh about the possibility of reserving a room with a two-story hot tub in the shape of a champagne glass. There are his and hers staircases leading to the top. On the way home, we get lost trying to find a secluded Christmas-tree farm that serves hot cider next to a bonfire. Eventually we give up and buy a precut tree from a parking lot in Bethlehem. We laugh about this, too.

I agree to go to First Presbyterian on Sunday nights and supervise a group of rambunctious ninth-grade boys. The youth pastor introduces me as an Iraq war veteran. She says, "God help you guys." We read the book of Acts. In chapter 16, Paul and Silas are dragged before a crowd, beaten, taken to prison, and placed in chains. An earthquake destroys the prison and frees the prisoners. The prison guard, having failed to do his job, tries to kill himself. The ninth-grade boys aren't paying attention. They're throwing doughnut holes at each other. One ricochets off an empty chair and lands in my lap. One boy says, "Oh, shit, he's going to kill you."

One of the other ninth-grade boys says, "My dad says you were in Iraq. Did you get shot at?" So I tell stories about convoys and land mines, mortars and rockets, gunfire and prisoners. Some of the stories are true. The boys love the ones that aren't.

I request a deferment from the seminary. The deferment policy says something about family emergencies, so I tell the seminary I'm having a family emergency. I tell them my heart condition has worsened and I'd like to take a year to focus on treatment. This is a lie.

I don't know anything about my heart. I haven't seen a cardiologist since leaving the NSA. I have no intention of seeing one in Bethlehem. But it's a convenient excuse to take a year off in Bethlehem and focus on the things I enjoy.

There are fewer arguments and fewer fights at home. I read books in front of the wood stove. We have the rambunctious ninth-graders over to watch the Super Bowl. The nightmares recede. I drink less alcohol. And then I write an article for the newspaper about Iraq, and Karin and I discover that we aren't back yet.

11

The Philadelphia Inquirer

SEPTEMBER 7, 2006

There's a large pool of blood on the floor. I'm aware that it's part of a dream, but I can't wake up. The blood slides toward my feet. My legs are sluggish and I can't get out of the way. The puddle moves as if it's alive. It nips at my feet as I pull back in fear.

I wake up. I'm afraid to go back to sleep.

That dream came to me almost every night when I returned from Iraq in the summer of 2004. It was just one of a series of nightmares that visited me on a consistent basis. The longer I was home, the less frequent the nightmares became, but they never completely stopped. They return without warning. I'm convinced they'll never be gone for good.

I was a civilian contractor in Iraq from December 2003 to May 2004. I served as an intelligence specialist in Abu Ghraib, Fallujah and Baghdad. My ability to speak Arabic made me a valuable commodity and allowed me to work directly with Iraqi citizens. A few of them inevitably became my friends. During a rocket attack one afternoon at Camp Victory in Baghdad, two of them were killed.

I retrieved their bodies from the U.S. military morgue the next morning. I was to meet the families at the front gate and notify them of the deaths. The body bags were not labeled, and I was forced to make identifications, but the men were so disfigured, I couldn't tell the difference between the two. I unzipped the bags and searched the bodies for ID cards. Blood poured out of one of the openings and streamed to the floor. It covered my boots. It's the same pool of blood that visits me in my nightmare.

This is one of the untold stories of the war in Iraq. It is an example of the scars and the wounds about which no one wants to hear. Instead, we focus on the more than 2,600 deaths and argue about what they mean. Some think of them as a reasonable sacrifice for the greater good, while others consider them a terrible crime. But no one wants to think of the damage that's been done to those who have returned home. We call those who served heroes and throw them a barbecue. We tell them we'll take care of them.

I don't know how many are suffering from their memories of Iraq. Maybe I'm the only one. Common sense tells me otherwise, but I can speak only of my own pain. It is severe, but I usually share it with no one. I'm embarrassed at times, fearing I'm the only one who has been unable to control it. As a man who has served as a soldier and worked as a police officer, I should be immune to such fears. I should be able to control my emotions and move on without complaining. That's no longer working.

I am quick to anger now, and my temper flares without much reason. I cry without cause, and I struggle to find purpose in everyday tasks. I used to value hard work; now I feel lazy. I've found ways to go on with life, hide the symptoms, and pretend nothing is wrong. For now, no one can tell the difference.

I listen as others debate the war in Iraq and talk about what it has cost. They wonder how it will affect elections and gas prices. They compare it with wars of the past and disagree about how much tougher or easier this one has been. They argue about phrases like civil war and accuse one another of making mistakes. In the end, though, they always say they support the troops. It brings consensus and makes them feel as though they're doing their part. They move on to the next topic.

I can't find a way to move on. There is no way to change what Iraq has done to me. The scars are permanent, and I've grown tired of hiding them. It's time for the nation to start thinking about what it really means to support those who serve. It's time to consider the full effects of this war on the nation's sons and daughters. The experience doesn't end once you're home. In many ways, it's just beginning. While the rest of the nation sleeps soundly tonight, I'll go back to my nightmare in Iraq.

Eric Fair

The piece is well received. I get emails. Nice ones. Ones that say, "I hope you sleep better," and "Don't feel guilty," and "Anything we can do?"

A professor from Villanova who teaches an introductory writing class asks me to answer her students' questions about writing and war. One student writes about her father. He died a few years ago. He was a Vietnam veteran. He never spoke about his experiences. She wants to know why I have gone public with mine. Why not get the help I need in private? Why not keep it to myself? Why am I seeking attention?

The professor calls and thanks me for taking the time to respond to these questions. She says the students were impressed that a writer would send personal emails. She says the students were particularly impressed with the way I handled the questions from the student who questioned my motivations. She says every class has one of these students. She says, "The rest of them know you weren't trying to impress anyone."

The student who questioned my motivations is right. I was trying to impress everyone. The piece is deceptive. It says nothing about interrogation and nothing about torture. It says nothing about the old Iraqi man I shoved into the wall. It makes it sound as though the two boys were my friends. I alter the story about returning to the same body bag, but only to simplify the narrative. Nothing in the article is meant to be untrue, but the picture it paints is an absolute lie.

I haven't yet mustered the courage to confess, so I hide behind a story meant to impress.

Still, the piece in the *Philadelphia Inquirer* sets me in motion. I'm not sure what would have happened if I hadn't published that first article. I might very well have found a way to bury my experience in Iraq. I might even have found a way to feel good when people thanked me for my service. But in late 2006 I started a process I wasn't able to stop.

Many of the people who respond to the essay encourage me to publish more articles, and while they can't possibly know the real story that needs to be written, their voices contribute to a call to start moving forward. So I keep writing.

11.1

At night, in bed, Karin and I talk about starting a family. We've had this discussion before, during our engagement, while we were walking around a kettle pond on Cape Cod. We agreed to have children, but not right away. We haven't talked about it since. For a time, after I was diagnosed with heart failure, Karin wouldn't sleep with me, afraid that I would suffer cardiac arrest in the middle of sex. That never happened, but we agreed the heart condition changed our views on family. Then there was Iraq. That changed our views as well.

We've been married five years. I'm thirty-four. Karin is thirty-two. We're older than our parents were when we were born. We both agree the time is right. Karin is comfortable in her position as an engineer. We're both becoming more comfortable with the idea of moving to Princeton for seminary in the coming year. We agree it would be a great place to raise a child. In the meantime, I write more articles for newspapers.

In December 2006, someone sends me a link to an op-ed in the *New York Times*. The piece, which was published nearly a year earlier, is by Tony Lagouranis, an Army interrogator who served in Iraq in 2004. The piece is called "Tortured Logic." It details his experiences in Iraq and questions the efficacy of aggressive and abusive interrogation techniques. I'm familiar with most of these techniques. I used many of them and had success with them. In the email, a sentence from the piece is highlighted.

> Perhaps, I have thought for a long time, I also deserve to be prosecuted.

The email asks, "Did you know this guy?"

I did not know Tony Lagouranis. But I know his experiences. I know why he questions what he deserves. I know why he questions why some were held accountable and others not. I know why he feels he did something wrong, and I know why he wonders whether he should be prosecuted.

When I read Lagouranis's essay, I am ashamed.

11.2

On December 11, 2006, I submit an opinion piece to the *Washington Post* about interrogation. Four days later it is accepted for publication. I tell Karin there will be consequences for making my Iraq experience public. I say, "People aren't going to be happy." She says, "As long as you think it's the right thing to do."

Karin and I sit in the house on Bonus Hill and have one of the first discussions about Iraq either of us can remember. I admit for the first time that I hung up on her from Abu Ghraib, that hearing her voice was just too painful, that somehow it made me realize I was doing something wrong. So I shut her off. Karin tells me how she felt helpless, how everything she did seemed wrong, how there was nothing she could do for me from home. But she promises to stand behind me now. She doesn't care what anyone else thinks. It's the right thing to do.

In late 2006, writing an article about something like sleep deprivation is dangerous. Many Americans are still under the impression that the abuse of Iraqi prisoners at Abu Ghraib was an isolated incident in an otherwise well-run detention program. Two more years will pass before the vice president of the United States tells the world that he ordered waterboarding. Two years will pass before he says, "I thought it was absolutely the right thing to do." Eight years will pass before the U.S. Senate releases a report on torture and the country learns about the technique called rectal rehydration.

But in 2006, I think I may go to jail for what I am about to say. And I think it is exactly what I deserve.

11.3

The *Washington Post* piece appears on February 9, 2007. In it, I describe nightmares and screaming, and I make reference to sleep deprivation in Fallujah. I say I witnessed and participated in other abuses as well, and I'm struggling with the consequences of my actions. I say that oppressive prisons create enemies, and that there is more to be learned about what went on at Abu Ghraib.

The piece appears on the *Post*'s website the night before it goes to print. Karin and I sit in bed with our separate computers and monitor the newspaper's homepage. My essay appears just before midnight. The first email message appears at 12:20 a.m. It says, "Thank you."

When we wake up the next morning there are more than two hundred messages in my in-box. One of them asks, "Are You Gay?"

Karin wakes up for work. We have breakfast and laugh about the email questioning my sexuality. We read it over and over again.

Eric,

   I just read your sad story. You sound like Richard Simmons. Butch
up, Sally.

At noon, I receive a phone call from Army CID. They want to
come speak with me in Bethlehem. They'll be out first thing tomorrow morning. It's a Saturday. I stop answering emails.

11.4

The next morning, ten minutes before the appointment time, the CID
agent calls and asks that we conduct the interview at the local police
station. He's using "change of scenery," an interrogation tactic. I
used it at Abu Ghraib.

   I ask which police station. He says, "Bethlehem." I say, "Town-
ship or city?" He doesn't know. He pauses, tells me to hold on for a
minute, and then asks someone where he is. I recognize the voice in
the background. It's the supervisor of the records room at the Bethlehem Police Department. The CID agent asks whether I need directions. I say, "No, I've been there before."

   A friend connects me with a lawyer. The lawyer offers to accompany me to the police station. I decline. He says, "Don't sign anything." I thank him for the advice. For the first time since losing my
job to a heart condition, I return to the City of Bethlehem Police
Department.

11.5

At the front desk, I sit and talk to the sergeant on duty. He was one of
my training officers, one of the good ones. We talk about the current
condition of the police department and the number of new officers

who have been hired. We talk about the CID agent. He says, "How much longer should we make the asshole wait?"

I meet the CID agent in one of the interview rooms in the back of the station. Police headquarters is in the basement of city hall, so there are no windows in any of the rooms. He asks me to close the door. I decline. He says it will be easier to conduct the interview with the door closed. I ask him whether I'm under arrest.

The door remains open and the interview proceeds. When it's over, the agent hands me a pamphlet entitled "Initial Information for Victims and Witnesses of Crime." He says, "I'm required to give this to you." I read the first paragraph:

> Introduction: We are concerned about the problems often experienced by victims and witnesses of crime. We know that as a victim or witness, you may experience anger, frustration, or fear as a result of your experience. The officer responsible for Victim/Witness Assistance at your installation can help.

11.6

When I get home, I speak with the lawyer again. I tell him I didn't sign anything in my meeting with CID. I tell the lawyer I intend to cooperate. He says this is the right thing to do, but he also says it makes sense for me to have legal representation. He says, "Rest assured, these guys don't care what happens to you."

The CID agent calls again. He wants me to come to Washington, D.C. The Department of Justice wants to talk to me. He says, "This thing goes all the way to the top." I call the lawyer back.

In Washington, I meet with the lawyer in his office on K Street. The law firm is enormous. It occupies multiple floors. Two lawyers are assigned to my case. They will walk me through the initial stages of the process. If it goes to trial, a new team will be assigned. The head of the law firm stops by to pay a visit. He says I have nothing to worry about and I should listen to his lawyers. He says, "None of our clients have ever gone to jail."

We take a break. The lawyers order lunch. They sit with the head of the law firm and talk about their families. They talk about a search committee and a new pastor. The head of the law firm and one of the lawyers attend the same church. They are Presbyterians.

The lawyers arrange a meeting with representatives of the Department of Justice. I agree to cooperate with the U.S. attorney's office for the Eastern District of Virginia.

11.7

I spend the spring of 2007 dealing with the fallout from the *Washington Post* piece. By May, I've received more than three thousand emails. The op-ed appeared on numerous blogs and was reprinted in a number of newspapers and publications throughout the country. Messages from readers continue to flow in. Someone sends me *Rolling Stone*. There's a chart called "Threat Assessment." It's inserted into an article about the decline of evangelical Christians in politics. The left side of the chart is labeled "With Us." The right side of the chart is labeled "Against Us." I'm number two on the "With Us" side, just below the North Dakota Senate, which has voted to repeal a 117-year-old law that made premarital cohabitation a sex crime. Just below me on the "With Us" side is Karl Rove, who endorsed illegal immigration by saying, "I don't want my seventeen-year-old son to have to pick tomatoes or make beds in Las Vegas."

An email from the office of former president Bill Clinton arrives, asking for my home address. A week later, Bill Clinton sends me a handwritten note. He uses the word "courage."

But despite all the praise and attention, I know that the op-ed is not courageous. It is cowardly. Every word, every phrase, and every sentence was crafted to ensure that I did not implicate myself in anything criminal. I provided no names, no specific dates, and no specific locations. The techniques I mentioned were taken straight from the interrogation handbook or from the list of approved "enhanced interrogation techniques." While I question the morality of my behavior, I do not call for my own prosecution. By my own account in the article, I've done nothing wrong.

As email messages lauding my honesty and courage continue to arrive, I delete them. But there is another kind of email I can recognize by the subject line. Instead of phrases using words like "courage," "honesty," and "hero," there are phrases like "I hope you die." I don't delete these emails. I read them over and over.

An email arrives that says, "Welcome."

Welcome to the club brother.

I was in the infantry in Vietnam in 1968. I murdered an NVA soldier who was trying to surrender. I gave the go ahead for two of our artillerymen to gun down these two soldiers. All I had to do was tell them not to but instead said, "Fuck it!" This has been a burden for thirty-nine years and will continue to be so until I die. I don't believe in any religion, I do believe in an Infinite Intelligence and perhaps our punishment is carrying this guilt to our graves. I just want to let you know you have plenty of company. Welcome.

At First Presbyterian Church in Bethlehem, a pastor preaches a sermon about the importance of legacy. He talks about how God works generationally. The consequences of our actions in life are laid upon our descendants. Some families are rewarded, while others are punished. He tells a story about Al Capone's lawyer. The lawyer helped keep Capone out of jail. This made him bad. Later, the lawyer had a crisis of conscience and decided to testify against Capone. This made him good. As a reward, God bestowed a heroic legacy upon the lawyer's son who joined the Navy, became a pilot, and shot down Japanese planes during World War II. Eventually the son was shot down too. He died. They named the airport in Chicago after him.

Karin says, "Is that a punishment or a reward?" I say, "Maybe we shouldn't have a child after all."

The good days in Bethlehem were short. They ended when I starting writing articles. I'd stopped drinking for a time, but I'm an alcoholic now. I don't sleep. I yell a lot. Mostly at Karin. But at other people, too. I have no job, and no interest in finding one. I rarely attend church. When I do, I'm hungover. At night I think about dying. I wonder how much longer my heart will last. I wonder whether I'll know the time has come or whether I'll just shut off. I wonder whether Ferdinand felt anything, whether he knew. I think about the mortar attack in Fallujah, when Ferdinand pretended he was trying to catch the incoming rounds. He said his death would be a mercy killing. I wonder whether he was relieved when the time came.

Like the decision to leave the NSA, the decision to finally go to seminary in Princeton is made out of desperation. I am unstable. I've made Karin unstable, too. Karin got pregnant during the good days in Bethlehem, but the good days are gone now. We should stay where we are and search for stability. We should focus on our family. We should focus on each other. But we make another mistake and move to Princeton.

12

___

In June 2007, I enter Princeton Theological Seminary's administration building to file paperwork for my veterans benefits. I am early. The office is closed. Other students wait with me. I avoid them. I look at the pictures on the walls. They are black-and-white, taken during the Civil War. There is a grainy photo of Brown Hall with a blurred image of a student walking across the quad. I wonder whether he is a veteran of Antietam or Gettysburg. I wonder whether he knew Andersonville or Camp Douglas.

In a summer language class, I study Greek in order to read the New Testament more effectively. It reminds me of DLI. I settle into a life of muggy morning walks to class, followed by chilly afternoons in the seminary library. I arrive on campus in the early morning, review my homework, attend class, eat lunch in downtown Princeton, and then spend the rest of the afternoon memorizing verb charts and case endings. I return home in the early evening, tell Karin about the day, eat dinner, watch the news, get drunk, and read emails with subject lines such as "Iraq," "interrogation," and "torture."

Mr. Fair, I still have a .45 caliber 1911. I suspect you know the firearm. I'd loan it to you gleefully if you get really depressed. And

I'd happily take whatever legal consequence might come my way
for having done so. You'd be doing the world a favor by removing
yourself from the gene pool. With revulsion at the subhuman you
and others like you surely are.

Karin is keeping her job as a chemical engineer. The company
allows her to work from the apartment in New Jersey. Occasionally,
she travels back to the home office in Allentown for meetings. She
spends the night with friends or family. I enjoy the time she is gone.
I pretend I'm not married. I pretend I've just graduated from Boston
University in 1994 and I've gone directly to seminary. There has been
no Army, no police department, and no Abu Ghraib, just a calling to
be a pastor. Maybe I'll marry another seminary student. We'll work
together at a Presbyterian church where she can run the children's
ministry, and I can do something like missions or outreach. But Karin
eventually comes home. She looks pregnant now. Our son is due to
be born in a few months.

As Greek consumes my mornings and afternoons in Princeton,
Iraq dominates what remains of my day. I return home to the apartment and field phone calls from reporters in Philadelphia, filmmakers
from Norway, psychologists from Boston, authors from the world
of academia, and lawyers looking to sue interrogators who abused
detainees in Iraq.

The lawyer from Washington calls. He has scheduled a meeting
with the Department of Justice and CID. He managed to secure a
limited type of immunity for the meeting. He calls it "queen for a
day." He faxes me a letter from the government.

You have advised me that your client, Eric Fair, wishes to meet
with the government for the purpose of making a proffer related
to allegations of detainee abuse under investigation by the United
States Attorney's Office for the Eastern District of Virginia. In the
event that your client is prosecuted by this office, the government

will not offer as evidence in its case-in-chief or at sentencing any statements made by your client at the meetings, with the following exceptions:

There are two pages of exceptions.

I tell my professor I am sick. I put away verb charts, lists of participles, and lexicons and board a train for Washington to meet with lawyers and CID agents in the shadow of the U.S. Capitol. I disclose everything. I provide pictures, letters, names, firsthand accounts, locations, and techniques. I talk about Randy Kutcher, Mike Henson, John Blee, and Michael Bagdasarov. I talk about Brent and Jim. I talk about Tyner and Hoagie. I talk about Dent. I talk about Ferdinand. I talk about the hard site at Abu Ghraib, and I talk about the interrogation facility in Fallujah. I talk about what I did, what I saw, what I knew, and what I heard.

I mention the Palestinian chair. I tell the story about the mayor of Fallujah and what it looked like to see him sitting in the chair. One of the CID agents is skeptical. He says maybe I just didn't understand what was going on. He was in Iraq, too. He conducted interrogations. He says he worked in austere environments. Sometimes they had to build their own furniture. He wonders whether this was the case in Fallujah. I say, "Are you suggesting it was just a poorly constructed piece of furniture?"

I show them the photograph of me in Fallujah, crouching down next to the chair. The CID agent says, "Okay, I get it."

The lawyer from the Department of Justice asks questions about Sergeant Hoagie. He wants to know more about the time Hoagie slapped a detainee. He says, "Was it an open-handed strike? Are you sure he didn't close his fist? What did it sound like when he hit him, a thump or a slap?" He returns to these questions time and again. He's frustrated. At the end he says, "There's nothing here, we don't have anything."

My lawyers are happy. They say the meeting went well. They say I did well. I was honest and engaging. They say I even managed to win over the angry CID agent. They say, "By the end, they were even starting to like you."

I am not prosecuted. No one from CACI is prosecuted. Nothing we did in Iraq was illegal. We tortured people the right way, followed the right procedures, and used the approved techniques. There are no legal consequences.

I ride the train back to Princeton. I start drinking more.

12.1

In September, there is an orientation weekend for the incoming class. We attend a chapel service, a speech by the dean, and a barbecue. At the barbecue, I meet Austin Ashenbrenner. He reminds me of Ferdinand. We become friends.

Austin grew up in Oregon and attended a Presbyterian church. There are Presbyterian pastors in his family. He likes church services with organs, not overhead projectors. He attended George Fox University, a Christian school in Oregon. After college he worked in youth ministry. Austin made the right choices, listened to the right voices, followed the right path. He will be a Presbyterian pastor. I will not.

Austin and I attend a peace rally at the seminary. It has something to do with torture. One of the professors running the event has read my op-ed in the *Washington Post*. It's the first time I agree to speak publicly at the seminary about my experiences in Iraq. The audience is made up of seminary students. I'll be attending class with them in the coming days. I give my speech.

I go home and read more emails.

Mr. Fair, your words are empty and hollow. I do not accept a single one of them. But let me offer you a suggestion if you want to do the honorable thing: kill yourself. Leave a note. Name names.

Until that day, I hope you never sleep another hour for the rest of your life.

When the fall semester begins, I join one of the seminary's flag football teams. The league is in need of referees. I agree to volunteer. I show up for a game, don my striped shirt, and blow the whistle. Players from both teams are furious. I am a terrible referee. One player approaches me, grabs my shirt, pulls me toward him, and then shoves me to the side. "See, see, this is what they're doing. They can't do this. It's called holding."

In Fallujah, I am grabbing a detainee, shoving him to the side, moving him through the line of Iraqis just taken from the battlefield. Some are still bleeding. One is missing part of his face. Well-dressed ones to the right, shabby ones to the left, faceless ones to the medic. The well-dressed ones are likely men of influence. The shabby-looking ones are the pawns. But the shabby ones never seem to understand directions. They just stand there looking dumb, so I grab them and shove them and push them.

I consider the student who shoved me. My heart is racing. I feel it struggle and thump inside my chest. I breathe the right way to get it back under control and I let the student walk away.

At the apartment, I yell. I yell about the student who shoved me and how I will kill him. I yell about other things too. Eventually I turn on Karin and start yelling at her. I say something terrible. I leave to buy whiskey.

12.2

In November 2007, I sleep in Karin's hospital room at Princeton University Medical Center's maternity ward. My newborn son sleeps in a small crib at the foot of Karin's bed. He is two days old. Karin is recovering from a Caesarean section. I wake up and look at my son, and I think I've made a mistake. I think the decision to start a family is another wrong path; a symptom of my instability, another poorly planned transition, another closed door. These are terrible thoughts, but they wash over me uncontrollably. It occurs to me for the first time that I am sick in a way that has nothing to do with heart failure. I am lost, and I will never get back. I need to get out of the way.

In Karin's room in the maternity ward, with my son lying at her feet, I think it is time to kill myself. I am interfering with too many other lives, too many other paths. I've been in Karin's way for years, holding her back, preventing her from moving forward while I looked backward and tried to salvage what was already gone. I do not want to be in my son's way. I do not want to interfere with his path. It is time to die. My son is two days old when I hear my first call to suicide.

12.3

In the spring of 2008, I attend a conference entitled No2Torture at Columbia Theological Seminary in Georgia. The conference is attended by notable members of the anti-torture movement within the Presbyterian church. The speaker list includes Lucy Mashua, a torture survivor from Kenya. She endured female circumcision along with additional abuse for speaking out. She is there to speak for the victims of torture. I am there to speak for those who tortured them.

Everyone else at the conference is defined by a stance against interrogation and torture. Some have written books or published academic papers; some for nonprofits. They know a great deal about the Geneva Conventions, or the United Nations Convention Against Torture, or even the Army's field manual on interrogation. In fact, they know a great deal more than I do about the legal definition of torture and the country's policies on interrogating detainees.

We break into small groups. Each group has a large placard identifying its purpose. My placard reads "Victims and Perpetrators." Lucy, the victim, sits across from me. We are surrounded by other participants who want to hear what Lucy and I have to say. We say nothing. A photographer approaches. We stand for a picture. People gather to watch. Someone says it is a vision of heaven: victim and torturer hand in hand. We are not hand in hand.

Back at Princeton, Karin and I sit in front of our apartment with our young son. Another couple walks by with their two-year-old boy. The husband is a teaching assistant in one of my classes. They stop to talk, and in the background, the two-year old stands by the side of a busy road, drops his pants, and urinates on a large sycamore tree. The parents are embarrassed. They have just returned from a weekend camping trip where his father taught the son how to pee in the woods. I say, "He's just following orders."

A few minutes later, the mailman comes by and hands us a batch of magazines and letters. There's a postcard from one of Karin's friends who works for the State Department in Kenya. The postcard is a photograph of him dancing with a group of Kenyans dressed in traditional clothing; his arms are thrown in the air, his legs lifted off the ground. Karin hands me the picture and laughs. She says, "There's something you're not cut out to do."

I yell. Although I have yelled at Karin before, it's never been like this. I am wild and full of rage. I see fear in Karin's eyes, and it makes me angrier. I tell her it is her fault for making me angry. It is her fault that she is afraid. I say, "Who the fuck are you to tell me what I can't do?" We go inside, where the yelling continues. My son is crying. I put him down for a nap and return to yell at Karin.

The next day, when I'm sober, I concede that I cannot be a Presbyterian pastor. I concede that I can't fix what went wrong at Abu Ghraib. I concede that I need to start letting other people tell me what I can and can't do. Karin says, "Let's just go home."

12.4

Near the end of the spring semester in 2008, as Karin and I are making arrangements to move back to Bethlehem, the dean sends me an email. An alumnus of the seminary has read my articles and heard an interview I did with a local NPR station. Apparently I said something worrisome about anger and alcohol. The dean copies two of her secretaries on the message. I don't know the secretaries. In the email, the dean says the alum is concerned about my safety as well as the safety of other students at the school. The alum wanted to make sure everyone was safe, so he asked the dean to contact the office of student counseling to be sure I was getting the help I needed. She did. The dean says that normally things wouldn't work this way, but "your case is unique."

The dean has no right to ask whether I'm in counseling. It's an incredible breach of trust. She has even less right to reveal my counseling status to other employees of the seminary. It's unprofessional. It would be an embarrassing oversight at any place of employment. At a seminary, it's inexcusable.

I'm furious. But I'm angry all the time now, so I'm not sure whether my anger is related to the email or just my usual condition. I know Karin shies away from confrontation, but I also know she is capable of nothing but honesty. She may hold back and say nothing in order to avoid confrontation, but she'll never make something up. So I show her the email from the dean and ask her what she thinks. To my surprise, she is furious. She is angry for me, and she is on my side. I call my counselor. I leave a message. I say, "I have some concerns. And Karin does, too."

The seminary agrees to set me up with a private practice in Princeton. They cover the costs. The practice conducts an intake interview. The head counselor calls the next day. She offers to see me personally.

We leave Princeton in June and return to Bethlehem. The dean's email serves as a convenient excuse when people ask why I left seminary, but in truth it had nothing to do with the decision. I'm not sure what there is for us in Bethlehem, or what will come next, but at least Karin will be near family and friends. I don't know how to stop drinking and I don't know how to stop thinking of my son as just another closed door. I don't know how to move forward. But I know that Karin stood behind me at seminary when the people who should have been caring for me abandoned that responsibility. As everything else begins to collapse, Karin steps forward to protect me.

13

In 2010, Karin and I drive to the south side of Bethlehem to visit a friend. We drive past a portion of the old steel mill that is decorated with Chinese writing. Hollywood used the buildings while filming *Transformers: Revenge of the Fallen* in 2008. The filmmakers needed an appropriate setting to re-create a deteriorating Chinese industrial site. Army Blackhawk and Apache helicopters flew over the Lehigh River. Simulated explosions lit up the old blast furnaces. Actors dressed like soldiers ran down the streets. For a few nights, Bethlehem sounded like Iraq.

We pass by the old ore crane that still dominates the landscape near the river. My four-year-old son thinks the crane looks like an old railroad bridge. He likes the big red neon sign on the crane that says "Sands." The casino attracts Chinese immigrants from New York City who ride the bus to Bethlehem. The bus companies offer complimentary tokens for the casino, but the Chinese immigrants don't use the tokens. They spend the night in the bus terminal, sleeping in the shadows of the old blast furnaces, then ride the buses back to their neighborhoods and sell the tokens. None of them spend money in Bethlehem.

13.1

At First Presbyterian Church, our son sits between us. He is five now. We do not send him to the nursery or Sunday school. I don't know what they'll teach him there, and I want him to learn how to worship in the sanctuary. I want him to know how to sit still for an hour, sing the old hymns, experience the liturgy, and learn the Lord's Prayer. I want him to be comfortable in the quiet. I want him to be Presbyterian.

The Presbyterian Church (U.S.A.) is considering changing its rules to allow for the ordination of gay pastors. This makes me proud, but a number of Presbyterian congregations are unhappy with the change. The First Presbyterian congregation in Bethlehem is one of them. They're considering the first steps associated with leaving the denomination.

I attend a town hall meeting at the church with my father. Like me, he is concerned that the church will leave the denomination. The voices that oppose gay pastors sound angry and unwelcoming. It doesn't feel like the church he has known for more than forty years. Grandmother is still alive. She is concerned as well. We agree that this is not the church of our ancestors.

Sometime later the church joins an organization called the Fellowship Community. It will not allow gay pastors. Karin and I send letters to the church. We rescind our membership. For the first time in twenty-six years, I am no longer a member of a Presbyterian congregation.

13.2

In the summer of 2010, I ride the bus to the Port Authority in NYC and attend my first class of New York University's writing workshop for veterans of Iraq and Afghanistan. I meet Matthew Mellina. He reminds me of Ferdinand. He is large and friendly. He is young, in his twenties, but he looks much older. Our sons are the same age. He and the mother are separated. We both did things in Iraq. We both write. We become friends.

Mellina writes a story about suicide. It's about a suicide he witnessed. He writes about riding on a train and ignoring the inquiries of a patriotic old man. I write a ghost story about victims of war. In the story, there's a government bureau responsible for assigning these ghosts to the men who killed them. I call it the War Ghosts Bureau. My ghost is the mayor of Fallujah. He rides with me on the bus out of the Port Authority.

Mellina and I go out for beer. He asks whether I'm okay. I don't look well. I look sick. He says, "You sure, brother?"

I go home to Bethlehem. I'm not okay. I call an ambulance. It takes me to the local hospital. The local hospital calls the Hospital of the University of Pennsylvania in Philadelphia. They tell them I don't look well. They tell them my ejection fraction is even lower than before. There are irregular heartbeats. They arrange for a transfer. In early 2012 a cardiologist in Philadelphia says, "Your time is just about up."

13.3

By May 2012, I've become a regular participant in the NYU writing group. At the end of the spring semester, NYU organizes a reading at the Kennedy Center in Washington. Prior to the reading we're required to submit our material for editorial review. The Kennedy Center sends me an email:

> Hi Eric,
>
> First, thank you for sending your writing selection. I thought it was outstanding work. That said, I am wondering if there is a way to change the words "shit," "fuck," and "tits." I have attached your piece with those words highlighted in yellow as a reference. We try to do

everything we can to keep these Millennium Stage performances at the Kennedy Center appropriate for all ages, but it is not always possible. Just let me know your decision by Tuesday morning.

The short story I submitted was about a young man struggling to integrate memories of Iraq into his everyday life. He gets baptized, he opens body bags, and he and his friends get drunk and practice committing suicide. Mellina wrote a short story about a friend who does kill himself. Matt Gallagher, who wrote a memoir about Iraq, wrote a short story about a mother whose son has committed suicide. Roy Scranton, a PhD candidate at Princeton University, wrote about an Iraqi girl named Nazahah who sees terrible things. Perry O'Brien, a conscientious objector, wrote about training rabbits to fight an insurgency.

We all receive similar emails from the Kennedy Center asking that we eliminate language inappropriate for young families. At the workshop, we don't always write about war, but when we do, it is inappropriate for young families. We all agree not to eliminate inappropriate language.

I leave Bethlehem and make my way to New York's Penn Station to catch Amtrak's Northeast Regional into Washington. I find Roy Scranton and Perry O'Brien waiting in the passenger lounge. Mellina and Gallagher meet us on the train. We commandeer a booth in the dining car and tell jokes about saying "shit," "fuck," and "tits" at the Kennedy Center.

Amtrak passes through Princeton, not far from the theological seminary. I think about spending time in the library and ignoring homework for my Old Testament or modern Christian history class. Instead, I wrote stories about Iraq, using words like "shit," "fuck," and "tits."

In the train, Gallagher reads the newspaper, where he comes across an article about Marines who took pictures of themselves urinating on dead Taliban. Mellina says, "We all have pictures of us in Iraq doing far worse things. We all have the dead-body photos. We all stood next to dead bodies and took a fucking picture." I don't have a dead-body photo, but I do have a photo of me crouching next to the Palestinian chair.

Mellina wonders whether Amtrak serves beer this early. A man in the booth next to us tells him yes. Mellina goes for beer. When he comes back, O'Brien is talking about the drugs the VA has prescribed for him. He's on a beta blocker. It lowers his blood pressure when he gets nervous. We all understand.

Mellina starts talking about suicide. He says to me, "It's not like you haven't considered it, right?" He starts saying "fuck" a lot. Mellina is loud. As the profanity increases and the volume rises, he begins to catch the attention of other travelers. I watch as a woman in another booth turns around to look at us. She does this a lot, and she doesn't look happy. By now, she must know we've been to Iraq. She wants to say something like "Excuse me, would you gentlemen please refrain from cursing so much?" She doesn't do this. She just keeps turning around every time Mellina says "fuck." She gets off the train in Baltimore.

We arrive at Union Station in Washington. I was here five years ago to meet with the team of lawyers on K Street. They escorted me to a federal building where I was grilled by the Department of Justice attorney and the duo from the Army's Criminal Investigation Command. I told them everything I had seen and done at Abu Ghraib and Fallujah. Today, Perry O'Brien and I share a cab and talk about the need to legalize marijuana.

The Kennedy Center puts us up at the Riverside Hotel. I settle in and walk to the Lincoln Memorial and on to the Vietnam Memorial. I visit World War II and Korea as well. I wonder what they'll do for Iraq. I wonder how contractors will be remembered. I wonder whether there will be something for Ferdinand.

There is a rehearsal at the Kennedy Center. We practice with the microphones in order to familiarize ourselves with the sound system. We line up in alphabetical order. I go first. I read my stories and say "shit," "fuck," and "tits." Middle school students are on a field trip. Someone complains. The organizers scurry to the soundboard and shut off the microphones for the rest of the practice.

When it comes time for the performance, large white signs are placed out front that read, "Tonight's Millennium Stage performance contains strong language and mature themes." As we wait backstage, Russian ballerinas pass through our green room. They'll be performing on the main stage tonight. We head outside to catch a glimpse of the gathering crowd. There are tuxedos and limousines and beautiful dresses. The ballet starts a half hour after our performance ends. The Kennedy Center suspects that many of the people attending the ballet will drift over to our performance. They tell us to expect a large crowd. There are seats for three hundred.

A Kennedy Center representative tracks us down and leads us to the stage. She says, "The crowd's a little thin tonight. Give it time." Mellina counts the people in the seats.

We read stories about opening body bags. We read stories about suicide. We read stories about military burials. We read stories about Iraqi girls. We read stories about insurgency. In the background, the tuxedos and beautiful dresses make their way to the auditorium. A few glance at the sign about mature themes. The Russian ballet is well attended.

13.4

In October 2012, Dorothy Fair, my Presbyterian grandmother, dies. I'm asked to speak at the memorial service. I return to First Presbyterian Church for the last time. The kind, handsome pastor from my youth sits in the pew behind my family. I struggle at the lectern. I say that God works generationally and this gives me hope. I hope that someday Grandmother's character will rise again in her descendants. We will see her generosity, her humility, her kindness, and her innocence in our children. We will see it in their children. My son is the only child to carry the Fair family name. I look at him. I hope all of this is true.

13.5

In Bethlehem, Karin and I talk about the heart transplant waiting list. The social worker has warned us about the amount of stress we'll need to endure. She said, "Sometimes, it's too much for a marriage to handle." Karin and I wonder whether stress has a saturation point. Can you reach a point where more stress doesn't matter? Or is it possible for things to get worse? Karin and I don't think things can get worse, but if they do, we agree, the marriage will come to an end. I don't have a job, and so I don't have my own medical benefits. I haven't worked consistently enough since leaving the police department to qualify for disability, and I only served five years in the Army, so the government owes me nothing. If Karin and I separate, I won't be able to afford the transplant and I'll die. If we stay together and I receive a transplant, the recovery may put too much strain on our marriage and we'll still be forced to separate. So I die in that scenario, too.

And somehow, we find this funny. And somehow, we take comfort in knowing things simply can't get worse. Things will still be terrible, but we've reached the bottom.

We spend weeks talking about the list. I tell Karin I don't want to die in a hospital.

13.6

In February 2013, Karin and I spend time in New York City with Matthew Mellina, and as always, he is funny, and we all feel better about how terrible things are. But on the way back to the Port Authority bus terminal, it becomes difficult for me to breathe. We are on Eighth Avenue, just south of Twenty-third Street; I see the entrance to the A, C, and E trains, but I'm afraid that if we go down the stairs I won't make it back up. I sit down on the sidewalk. Karin is with me and watches over me, and we find a way to laugh about dying on a street in New York. Mellina will have to come get my body. I eventually struggle to Port Authority and we ride the bus home to Bethlehem.

A few weeks later, Karin takes our son to her parents' house for the afternoon. I lie on the couch and feel what it's like to die. Every breath must be accounted for. Life is no longer automatic. I use the muscles in my chest and abdomen to force air in and out of my lungs. I can sleep for only minutes at a time, waking up and gasping for breath. And then there is a sensation; a desperate need to have someone in the room, a primeval cry to not be alone. I am dying, and I think only of Karin. I call her and beg her to come home. I tell her not to bring our son. She sits with me and rubs my back and we talk about saying good-bye.

The cardiologists said this would happen. They said I would begin to feel the end through a series of episodes. They prescribe powerful drugs to keep me on my feet, keep me alive long enough to have the transplant. A permanent intravenous line is stitched into my arm, allowing medicine to be pumped directly into my heart. I feel alive again, but the cardiologists warn me the improvement is only temporary.

13.7

In Bethlehem, I exchange emails with Seth Goren, the associate chaplain at Lehigh University. He's a rabbi and a single parent. He is gay.

Seth and I have coffee for the first time. He's read some of the articles I've written. He sits and listens while I talk about Abu Ghraib and how I struggled to reconcile the life of Jesus with a church that failed to speak out against war and all but encouraged me to go to Iraq. Seth asks, "Which voices from your church were telling you to go to Iraq? And why did you listen to them?" I tell him the voices were mostly my own. Seth tells me that maybe it is time I listen to someone who will give me better advice. We laugh about this, but both agree that we need a voice of accountability in our lives.

Seth and I meet weekly. We become close friends. We sit at his dining room table and practice Hevruta, a traditional Jewish text-based study done with a partner. We speak softly until his daughter falls asleep, then spend hours sharing ideas and telling each other our stories.

Seth and I discuss forgiveness. Christianity taught me that my own forgiveness could only be achieved through the crucifixion, and that nothing I do on this earth can substitute for the death of Jesus on the cross. People like Don Hackett certainly encouraged me to think about the process of reconciliation, and to seek the forgiveness of those I'd wronged, but true forgiveness was a gift from God, not something to be earned. The memories of Iraq make believing that impossible. I need to earn my way back. I need to pay a price. Seth says, "Yes, this is what's so strange about you guys. How can you not owe anything? Why would you want it to be so simple?"

Seth and I study Maimonides, taking turns to read aloud and share our thoughts. Seth chose Maimonides because he lays out one of the most extensive processes in the Jewish tradition for atonement. Maimonides says the transgressor is required to engage with the aggrieved persons, actively seek their forgiveness, and make restitution for harms done. God has a role to play, but largely for sins against God. The emphasis is on human-to-human interaction. The remedies are often described as lifelong pursuits. When it's my turn, I read the next passage.

> For example, a person is not forgiven until he pays back his fellow man what he owes him and appeases him. He must placate him and approach him again and again until he is forgiven.

I say, "I'm pretty sure I won't live that long."
Seth says, "That doesn't mean you're not obligated to try."

13.8

In May 2013, I find myself standing behind a Bethlehem police officer at Starbucks. He recognizes me. It's been eleven years. He says I
look thin. I say, "Heart failure." He says they all thought that was
bullshit. They assumed I left the department to go work for the CIA.
They heard about the Iraq stuff. No way you do that with heart failure. But now I look sick. Now he believes me.

   He asks about the articles I've written for the Bethlehem *Morning Call.* He wants to know when the next one will appear. He says
a few of the officers look forward to my articles down at the department. I say I know my opinions aren't too popular with most of the
guys. He says, "You'd be surprised. Keep writing."

13.9

In June 2013, I am flown by helicopter to the Hospital of the University of Pennsylvania. We fly above the Pennsylvania Turnpike. I
think of December 2003 and my father driving me to the airport in
Philadelphia for my first deployment to Iraq. I still remember telling
him it was a bad idea, and I still remember him opening the car door
and telling me to get back in. And I still wish I had.

   In the hospital, I interrupt Todd, another heart failure patient.
He's reading the Bible. I apologize and offer to come back later. He
says, "No, no, just reading Psalm Twenty-three. One of my favorites.
It calms me. It lets me know that God is in control."

   We take a walk down a narrow hallway on the hospital's elev-
enth floor. It's the Cardiac Care Unit. It's where you go to wait for a
heart when you're too sick to wait at home. As we walk, we push
our IV towers out in front of us. They're loaded down with bags of
intravenous fluids and medicines. Both of us are on a constant infu-
sion of a drug called milrinone. It's delivered through the permanent
line in our arms. Milrinone is a powerful and dangerous drug that

helps the heart beat more efficiently, but it has a shelf life. You adjust to it. Over time, you need more and more. Eventually, the dose maxes out. The benefits begin to fade. You die. Todd and I are on the maximum dose. We are fading. We need someone else to die.

I tell Todd about my son. He tells me about his daughters. We talk about how much we hate low-salt diets. Todd talks about how much he'll miss alcohol. Especially beer. He'll miss a good beer. He wishes he had had one last good drink before coming to the hospital. "Yes," I say, "that would have been nice." He talks about church. The five-minute walk exhausts us. We return to our individual rooms to rest.

On Wednesday, June 26, 2013, I'm moved to the intensive care unit. A catheter is inserted through my neck and into my heart. It's the end. The catheter delivers critical doses of medicine to the heart, but it won't last long, and it's dangerous, so I'm not permitted to move. I lie in bed and think about Ferdinand.

On Sunday, June 30, someone else dies. The heart is flown to Philadelphia. I'm taken to the operating room, where the nurse reviews my medical history. She says, "Glad you got the alcohol under control." There's a section on my overseas service. She says, "Iraq? You were there? What did you do?"

The anesthesiologist asks me about music. I say anything from the eighties. They give me medicine. I feel good. The Bangles sing "Walk Like an Egyptian."

13.10

I wake up. I think about Fallujah. I think I might be there. I'm scared. There are voices and shadows in the room. The voices tell me to calm down. The tube in my throat prevents me from asking about Ferdinand. I start to cry. The voice tells me I'm in the surgical recovery room at the Hospital of the University of Pennsylvania. I've been intubated. I've had a heart transplant. I need to relax.

I point my finger in the air and spell out a word. K-A-R-I-N.

I spend the next two weeks in the hospital learning to live with a new heart. There are instructions on how to take my medicines, how to avoid infections, and how to start walking again. There is pain, sadness, fear, and euphoria. There is morphine and Percocet. There are emails and voice messages and Facebook posts.

The senior pastor from the First Presbyterian Church in Bethlehem, the church where I no longer feel welcome, brings his son to see me in the hospital. With the exception of family, they are the only ones who find time to visit.

13.11

In September 2013, it's been two months since the transplant. I'm lucky. This is what I tell people when they ask me how I'm doing. Occasionally I complain about side effects, or the pain from the surgery. I get lightheaded if I stand up too quickly. I get nauseated if I take the stairs too fast. But I don't tell them about the real side effects. I don't tell them about the inability to sleep, about the constant nausea coupled with an insatiable desire to eat. I don't tell them about the diarrhea, about the time I shit my pants while waiting for my son's school bus to arrive. People say, "Yes, but at least you're alive, right?" I say, "Yes, at least I'm alive."

At night, I wonder how much longer I'll actually be alive. There are statistics worth consulting, but every case is different. This is what medical professionals say when I ask about the likelihood of living long enough to watch my son graduate from high school. They tell me to enjoy the present. "Every case is different."

13.12

In Bethlehem, I park at Sand Island and follow the short path down to the Lehigh River. It is night. The steel mill's old blast furnaces are illuminated by decorative colored lights designed to draw attention to a $70 million arts and cultural center scheduled to be built next year. I stand in the river's waist-deep water, where the current flows at a steady pace. There is a Para Ordnance .45 caliber handgun, a Canadian kit weapon modeled after Browning's 1911. There is one round. The river will clean what's left and prevent the weapon from endangering anyone who finds me. It is late. The blast furnaces go dark. The water is cold. I think of a heart that isn't mine. I think, This must be how it feels to be baptized as an adult.

13.13

In April 2015, my father sends me an email about our family's history. He has cancer now, so we're having more and more conversations designed to preserve memories and pass down legacies. His latest email includes an audio file of a conversation my grandmother recorded in 1977 with her aunt Annie. It's the first time I've heard my grandmother's voice in three years.

The recording was made in Altoona, an industrial town in the central part of the state that once built the great steam engines of the Pennsylvania Railroad. The railroad went bankrupt in 1970, most of the engine shops closed, and Altoona went into decline. Annie Campbell, my grandmother's aunt, was born there in the 1880s, near the beginning of the railroad's empire. But in 1977 she's declining, too, and is unable to make the trip to the Burd family reunion in Colorado. So my grandmother records her voice in order to preserve the Burd family history.

On the tape, she introduces my grandfather. Like Aunt Annie, he was too sick to travel to the reunion. Multiple sclerosis was beginning to take its toll. By the late 1970s, he was spending most of his time in a wheelchair. The disease would eventually attack his esophagus. In 1986, during my freshman year of high school, he choked to death on a piece of chicken. His funeral was well attended, and he was remembered as a kind and gentle man.

My grandfather calls himself "old man Fair" and sends warm greetings looking down from the hills of central Pennsylvania. The multiple sclerosis renders his voice weak and slow, but his humor and goodwill remain intact. In the background, my grandmother reminds him to say hello to Nancy and to thank his brother Fred for the reunion patch. She says the patch will be a big sensation on Phil's pajamas down at the veterans hospital.

The conversation with Aunt Annie covers a variety of topics. There are questions about what it was like growing up on the farm in Pennsylvania Furnace (dull), and how often the mail came (twice a day), and what it was like to see a car for the first time (not too scary).

And then there are stories about growing up as the daughter of a Presbyterian minister in the late 1890s. As one would expect, the memories are mixed. There are good memories about living in the manse and attending large Sunday dinners, but Aunt Annie also has much to say about how she dreaded Sundays and how difficult it was to endure long hours at the church. She was forbidden from taking walks or playing outside. Much of the time was spent in Sunday services, where at least, she said, she could find time to sleep.

I think about the Reverend Campbell's sermons and his continued insistence that good behavior was a pathway to a right relationship with God. I can imagine Aunt Annie being lectured about this, and I can imagine her frustration at being told how to act and what to do. I can imagine myself in this scenario, and I can imagine myself choosing to chart my own path and make my own way, and I'm ashamed that I didn't do better. I'm ashamed that I didn't act more like a Campbell, a Burd, or a Fair.

But then my grandmother asks Aunt Annie how she felt about living with a minister, and if the long hours at church and strong focus on rules made her a better person. Aunt Annie says they were expected to be good examples, except that they weren't. My grandmother laughs and says, "Oh, Aunt Annie." But Aunt Annie says, "We were just human kids. Not model kids by any means."

I'm relieved to hear Aunt Annie talk about not always being a good example. There are no dark secrets in my family, no sordid episodes that overshadow my own transgressions. Aunt Annie is not about to expose some sin to which I can relate. But when asked to reflect at the end of her life, she seems keen to point out that she fell short of expectations.

Aunt Annie said she was a human kid. I can't know exactly what she meant by this, but it leaves me feeling less isolated. It leaves me feeling as though there is still a place for me in my own family. It leaves me feeling as though I have not done something that can't be undone.

Not long after my grandmother died, Don Hackett asked me whether I still prayed. I do not. But unlike those mornings at Abu Ghraib when I avoided prayer in order to ignore my own failures, I avoid it now because I have a debt to pay, and I have no right to petition someone else to pay it. I am a torturer. I have not turned a corner or found my way back. I have not been redeemed. I do not believe that I ever will be. But I am still obligated to try.

13.14

On July 5, 2015, I board the Pennsylvanian, Amtrak's train from New York City to Pittsburgh, with my father and my seven-year-old son. We are going to Pittsburgh to see a Pirates game, but the train ride is the most important part. My father loves these trips. They remind him of his childhood in Altoona, surrounded by the steam engines of the Pennsylvania Railroad. Now he wants to pass that love down to his grandson before he is gone. I pretend the love of trains skipped a generation, but secretly, I love riding the rails more than anything.

The ride is long and the train is crowded; when we board, no one moves to offer seats together to a seven-year-old and his stay-at-home father. So we sit in aisle seats, two rows apart. Near the end of the trip, in the dining car, the old woman sitting next to my son approaches and compliments me on his good behavior. He has been sitting still, reading books, and staying quiet. He's been acting like a Presbyterian. My grandmother would approve. "He's unlike any seven-year-old boy I've ever seen," the old woman says. This makes me proud. But then she starts asking questions about me.

The old woman reminds me of my grandmother; she grew up in Latrobe, a town not unlike Altoona. She even sounds like my grandmother. She starts asking questions about family and where I live and where I was born. I want to talk about my son again, but, like my grandmother, she persists. She asks about the jobs I've had and the people I've known. She asks about what I've done.

In 2015, I should be telling stories about how I'm entering my fourteenth year with the Bethlehem Police Department. I'd be a detective, or a patrol sergeant, or maybe a seasoned beat cop content dealing with traffic violations and stolen bicycles.

Or, if I'd gone to seminary after college, I could talk about how I'm in my eighteenth year of ministry with the Presbyterian Church. I'd likely be leading a church of my own with the help of associate pastors like Austin Ashenbrenner. I think I would have been good at that. I think I will try that path again.

I'm still married. It's been thirteen years. I suppose, like most successful couples, we've survived by admitting we've failed. Karin and I have been to war against each other, and we are both casualties. But we sit together at night and find that there is still love there. We find that we are the same. We find there is no one who will ever understand us better.

Don Hackett used to tell me that the best way to hear God's voice is to seek out the silence. But there are so many voices now: the voice of the general from the comfortable interrogation booth, the cries from the hard site, the sobs from the Palestinian chair, and the sound of the old man's head hitting the wall in Fallujah. It is nearly impossible to silence them. As I know it should be.

I have not gone back to the Lehigh River with that gun in my hand. I hope I never do. But there are nights. Forgive me, there are nights.

I am just a human kid.

ACKNOWLEDGMENTS

This journey is not possible without the friendship of Matthew Mellina and Amy Cramer, the camaraderie of Matt Gallagher, Phil Klay, Maurice Decaul, and Roy Scranton; the instruction of Emily Brandt, Craig Moreau, Lizzie Harris, Maxim Loskutoff, and Eric Weinstein; the fellowship of Keith Brown, Walter Cramer, George Maunz, Tom Mics, and Jerry Scharff; the kindness of Kelly Denton-Borhaug, Daniel Jasper, and John Pettegrew; the care of Christine Gearhart, Ashley Wetherell, and Anjali Vaidya; and most important, the counsel and accountability of Seth Goren and Austin Ashenbrenner.

I am indebted to Nick Flynn and Bill Clegg for opening doors I had no right to pass through.

I am humbled by my editor, Sarah Bowlin, who had the courage to guide me on this path while still finding the strength to navigate her own.

I am grateful for Karin Fair, for staying on a path she did not choose, and had every right to abandon.

And for Aunt Penn, who bought me that book when I wanted that toy gun.

ABOUT THE AUTHOR

ERIC FAIR, an army veteran, worked in Iraq as a contract inter-rogator in 2004. He won a Pushcart Prize for his 2012 essay "Consequence," which was published first in *Ploughshares* and then in *Harper's* magazine. His op-eds on interrogation have been published in *The Philadelphia Inquirer*, *The Washington Post*, and *The New York Times*, among other places. He lives in Bethlehem, Pennsylvania.